FREE AT LAST!

My Journey Into, Through, and Out of Depression

MARILYN AVIENT

1st WORLD
PUBLISHING

Free At Last!

Marilyn Avient

© Marilyn Avient 2007

Published by 1stWorld Publishing
1100 North 4th St. Fairfield, Iowa 52556
tel: 641-209-5000 • fax: 641-209-3001
web: www.1stworldpublishing.com

LCCN: 2007929046

SoftCover ISBN: 978-1-4218-9975-6

HardCover ISBN: 978-1-4218-9976-3

eBook ISBN: 978-1-4218-9977-0

I lovingly dedicate this book to my parents,
Florence Gertrude Harback (née Gibson)
and Horace Richardson Harback:
"Mom and Dad,
we had some tough lessons to learn together,
but we did it!
I love you. I miss you."

To John,
for not leaving;
for showing me unconditional love;
for calling me "Princess".

To Sean and Jason,
"I'm sorry" is just not big enough!

To Lindsey,
for being there when I came out on the other side.

To Alexander, Amanda, Ben, Jenna, and Ysannah:
Five good reasons why I am glad that I
chose to be free at last!

ACKNOWLEDGMENTS

Irene,
you didn't know me at the time of this story, but you kicked my butt
until I finally wrote it. I couldn't have done it without you!

Pat,
you're my special girl! Love, Em

Sharon and Barbara,
we've been siblings all of our lives,
but we became sisters during a pedicure!

David,
you're the best brother, ever.
You always make me laugh but . . .
one day you touched my shoulder and let me cry.

Janet,
I knew from the beginning that you were right for Sean . . .
I just didn't realize *how* right!

Dan,
thank you.

Sally,
you have showed me how to be strong even
though the bottom of your world has fallen out from under you.
You're my hero.

Evelyn Perricone,
my wonderful editor!
Thank you for making this surprisingly long path a little less lonely.

All the good people at 1ˢᵗ World Publishing, especially
Ed Spinella, Mira Waller, and Rodney Charles.
I am proud to have worked with you.

A NOTE TO MY FAMILY

The contents of this book are solely presented from my vantage point.

The memories described are my truths and are honestly not meant to offend or hurt any of you. To tell my story, I had to tell it all and some of it is not pretty. No two people remember the same incident in the same way, so I can only tell my version and I hope that you will remember that as you read on. My fervent wish to all of you is that as you go through my book, you will also grow through it. I have written this book from a place of love. I hope that it will be received in that same way.

PREFACE

In 1984, I began a four-year odyssey through the mental health system. I was hospitalized on three different occasions for a total of 15 weeks, plus I spent 7 weeks in a mandatory day therapy program. Although I was treated with kindness and respect most of the time, there was very little concern about how, or why, I had come to be there. They asked me about my life at the time of the hospitalization, but little, if anything, was asked about my childhood once it was determined that I had not been abused or grossly mistreated. There was an over-all feeling of "if it is not overtly abusive, it is of no interest or consequence whatsoever." My psychiatrist said to me on one occasion, "I have no interest in your past, your future, or any-thing to do with your religious beliefs. Please limit our discus-sion to what has happened to you since your last appoint-ment."

Depression is still one of the most misunderstood medical conditions of our time—I know of few illnesses that are treat-ed with such complacency by the world at large. The symp-toms are described simply as follows:

* Sadness that has lasted longer than ten days
* Loss of appetite
* Reduced sex drive
* Difficulty making decisions

❧ Difficulty sleeping

❧ General disinterest in life

Anyone who has ever experienced the "pain" of depression knows it is often regarded with the same esteem given to premenstrual syndrome (PMS) or hypoglycemia, and we all know how much respect these receive. Depression has been dubbed the "Silent Killer," and yet people speak of it lightly and with little credibility. Many people think depression is a women's condition and some even go so far as to say it is a sign of weakness. Perhaps more women than men go for help when they are feeling so low, but this is definitely not a "female problem." And believe me—it is not for the faint of heart!

How many times have you heard someone say he or she is "so depressed" over something quite trivial—in the big scheme of things—like the weather, a promotion not coming through, or the fact that it is Saturday night and there is nothing to do? Some people even use it to merely describe that intolerable state of malaise some of us call *boredom*. *Depressed* is a word that is used carelessly and often without any thought or consideration for those who really are suffering from it. Depression is a condition that you might want to avoid telling your boss about; it could be the deciding factor on whether or not you ever get that promotion you have been waiting for so eagerly.

You never hear anyone lightly stating that he or she is feeling *diabetic* or *cancerous* because diabetes and cancer are seen with respect. When I was in the thick of my depression, I prayed for cancer, so that I could die in a way that would be acceptable by society's standards. Depression kills, but when it does, the person is seen as having taken the easy way out. Only those who have been in the severe throes of this condition know the horror of *pain of the mind*. I remember standing in my kitchen one day, holding my head, and screaming, "The pain!

Oh my God! Please make the pain go away."

In this book, I am simply telling my story with as much as honesty and integrity as memory will allow. I believe we each have a story and we each have our unique opportunity for growth—depression just happened to be my challenge of choice. You will read things about me that will make you shake your head in dismay and even disdain; believe me, upon remembering and then writing about them, I did much more than that.

My favorite therapist told me depression does not originate in the mind; rather, it is sadness of the soul. That makes sense to me. The sadness was within me from the time I was born and I desperately wanted to be consoled. Because I did not *listen* to my inner voice and its cries for help, I did not *hear* anything and therefore could pay no heed. Finally, after many years of getting no attention from me, my soul sent the pain to my emotional system and I experienced this as increased bouts of crying and moodiness. My family and friends described me as being overly emotional, overly reactive, and overly sensitive.

Still getting no active response to my escalating feelings, the sadness transferred to my mental system. Once there, it presented as panic attacks, confusion, overanalysis, and perfectionism. When these traits became commonplace, and in receipt of no special attention from me or anyone else, the final step had to be taken—the soul's sadness manifested itself in my physical body disguised as a chemical imbalance in my brain. This condition is very difficult to live with, so that is when I sought medical attention.

Psychologists may respond sooner, but generally the world of psychiatry is only willing to help once the brain and all its chemicals are brought into play. The first line of aid comes in the form of antidepressants, of which there are many varieties; in my case, it took a while to find one that actually worked for me. In 1984, I was diagnosed with bipolar affective disorder, more commonly known as manic depression. Over the years, besides many types of antidepressants, I was given sleeping pills, anti-anxiety pills, and Lithium, which was the standard medication for manic depression at that time.

Right or wrong, I went off all my pills in 1988, and please know that I am not recommending this to anyone else. By the time that it was necessary for me to go on medications again, in 2003, I was very thankful to learn that Lithium is rarely used anymore. The newer remedies have fewer, if any, side effects and do the job much more efficiently.

As a frontline defense, I have great respect for today's medications because they are generally affective in stabilizing the patient physically. When I was first hospitalized, I was too ill to deal with the mental, emotional, and spiritual causes of my breakdown, so the medications were helpful in bringing me back to life physically. I needed a rest from the demands of my world and the hospital stays gave me respite. However, as much good as these medications gave in bringing my brain back to working order, they did nothing to alleviate the original sadness of my soul.

I knew many patients who had little relief from antidepressants, so they were given electroconvulsive therapy (ECT)—the thought of which makes me cringe to this day. I remember the ECT patients standing at the elevator chatting quietly and looking fairly normal, then a couple of hours later they were rolled back to their rooms on gurneys, looking like they were returning from surgery. Later in the day, I would see them seeming anywhere from fuzzy and tired to spaced out. There was always a feeling of mystery around the ECT patients—like they knew something mysterious that I did not. After a few weeks some of them became brighter looking, but upon talking to them they would confess that they could not remember parts of their pasts. As the memories disappeared, so did their sadness. What does that tell you? The only positive thing that I will say about ECT is that each of them agreed that they experienced no pain during the procedure because they were well sedated—unlike the horror stories of pain from the early days of psychiatry.

The only male nurse on the ward told me, on my first night in hospital, that I would be wise not to entertain any high hopes of being cured. He explained that the mental health system is just one big revolving door. The patient comes into hospital, gets medicated, goes home, then comes back, gets medicated, then goes home again. The cycle continues ad infinitum. He sounded very bitter and very discouraged. (This was confirmed for me when one patient told me that she had been in hospital 10 times in half that number of years.) I was not surprised, a few years later, to learn that this particular nurse had gone into training to be a therapist because he felt, perhaps in that capacity, he would have more of a chance of doing some good.

In my years as a sufferer of depression, I experienced physical invisibility, extreme fear, and much loneliness because of my self-imposed seclusion. I know beyond a shadow of a doubt that there are many others out there who feel the same way, and I want to speak for them. I am telling my story in hopes that someone somewhere will read it and become more knowledgeable about this complicated and often misunderstood condition. I pray that by reading it, someone will feel more able to cope with the depressed person in his or her life. I pray that someone will read my story and, in turn, choose to deal with his or her own past. I pray that someone will read my story and will change how he or she thinks about this condition called depression. I pray that someone somewhere will read my story and will feel a little less invisible, a little less afraid, and a little less lonely. My story is "every story." The only difference between my story and theirs is that I am telling mine.

Author's Note: The organization of this book does not follow an exact linear timeline. Instead, it follows the causes and relevant effects of my inner problems and issues on the various important situations in my life. The narrative moves from the development of childhood fears and "survival rules"; to the turmoil of my teenage years and early adulthood; to my breakdown and years of coping with mental illness; to healing, revelation, and psychological growth; to lessons learned; and finally, to a satisfying sense of spiritual contentment.

In addition, throughout the book there are poems that were written by me in the years following my breakdown (1984–1992) and they are taken from my book of poetry called *The Girl Behind the Closed Door.* This book is my life in prose and that book is my life in poetry. As you will see, the "rhyming ditties" are strategically placed after the section about which they were written. I hope that they will bring another dimension to my story.

Marilyn Avient

PROLOGUE

November 15, 2002. . . I am launching my book, *The Girl Behind the Closed Door*. I cannot believe this night has finally arrived. As I sit in the green room (which is not green at all) waiting for my presentation to begin, I am amazed at how calm I feel. This feels so right. This feels so perfectly timed. This feels so exciting. I can hear the audience shuffling into the auditorium; once in a while I hear a voice that I recognize. The violins and the flutes of my favorite Celtic music fill me with joy and peace. My old friend, Beth, comes in to see how I am doing and we chat for moment. Beth was a source of strength for me in the early years of my depression and tonight I need her almost as much as I did then, but for different reasons. Tonight she is introducing me on stage because she is only one who has any idea how far I have come.

I tell her that my only fear is that I will cry and I do not want to do that because it will take away from the message that I am here to give.

She asks, "What is the most emotional thought you could have right now?"

I reply, "I want to make Judy proud."

Tears well up in my eyes, but I take a deep breath and will them to go away. Enough tears have fallen from these eyes and

I determine here and now that tonight is not the time for them. Tonight I am strong. Beth decides that maybe it would be best if she leaves me alone to just be with my thoughts.

As she goes out to start the introduction, I let myself feel the amazement of how I, who used to be afraid of my own shadow, am now going to get up before a crowd of people to tell intimate stories of my life. How did I get here? After traveling on the long and lonely road into depression, I found myself in a valley that was deep and seemingly inescapable. The one path out of the valley was steep, scary, and at times hopeless. Both roads had one thing in common—they all led me to this night, when I finally have a chance to shine. Tonight, it all makes sense. Tonight *the girl behind the closed door is free at last* . . .

FREE AT LAST

The gates are swinging open,
The barbed wire has lost its sting.
The chains are lying loose on the ground,
The birds feel free to sing.
I see the world before me
Just waiting with welcoming smiles.
I've waited so long for this moment,
For this, I have weathered the miles.
With baited breath I take one step,
Sounds simple, but so hard for me.
That step requires much courage,
I step past the gate and I'm free.
The birds sing out in triumph
A rainbow forms in the sky.
The four winds blow in harmony,
The sun gives a wink of his eye.
I see the crowd before me
They look so willing, so eager to learn.
I take a moment to say a short prayer.
Now I know why I had to return.

INTO . . .

I used to wonder where happiness is—
I searched and searched in vain.
I scanned the eyes and faces I loved
And explored the surrounding terrain.
No luck had I—it's all a myth—
No happiness to be found,
So I went inside to search my soul
Not knowing just where I was bound.

Excerpt from
"Happiness Where Are You?"
The Girl Behind the Closed Door
by Marilyn Avient

Marilyn Avient

CHAPTER 1

I, the girl behind the closed door, was born Judith Marilyn Harback, on February 16, 1948. My father gave me that name even though my mother had told him that she wanted me, her third daughter, named after her grandmother, so I was supposed to be Mary Ann. My dad never went against my mother's wishes, but this time he took it upon himself to do just that when he decided to name me Judith Marilyn. I have him to thank, and him to blame.

Judith became "Judy" and Marilyn sank into oblivion. I hated the name Judith and I detested the name Judy. They both felt awful to say and even worse to hear. I was always in dread of introducing myself to anyone because I honestly thought the name Judy sounded just plain goofy. I realized one day that a name actually identifies its bearer; if I hated my name, I hated myself. Finally, in 1996, I legally dropped the name Judith—thus Marilyn was born. This is our story.

Fear was my most faithful and most constant companion— day in and day out, in good weather, and in bad, for the vast majority of my life. I really cannot remember a time when I was not afraid of something. Every day I would wake up and see Fear sitting on the end of my bed, grinning at me in a most disturbing and patronizing way. I do not know why he even bothered to show up most days, because even without his presence I always gave in to whatever he wanted me to do; I was not a challenge to Fear in any way. Every day I was in "fight or flight" mode because every day I was filled with terror—the kind you have when, being chased by a herd of stampeding buffaloes, you come to a cliff and realize you have no choice except to jump; or when you are standing in the middle of the road and you see a truck speeding towards you, with no time to get out of its way. This feeling of adrenalin rushing though my body was never-ending and its power over me was unrelenting and exhausting. What was I afraid of?

The shorter list would be to tell you what I was not afraid of. I was *not* afraid of being murdered, raped, robbed, or mugged. I was not afraid of being bitten by a dog, stung by a bee, or involved in a traffic accident. I have healthy respect for these real fears and so I lock my doors at night, I drive with due caution, I make a practice of not sticking my nose into flowers, and I talk kindly to dogs.

The things that caused me great fear and panic were of the irrational variety and generally involved anything that made me feel out of control. I was deathly afraid of money and anything, or anybody, that had something to do with it such as bankers, lawyers, and accountants. When I was married to my first husband, Dan, I bounced a check for $100—my God, the shame of it! I timidly went to the bank to make good on the check and, to my embarrassment, I stood at the teller's window sobbing my heart out. Partly, I was angry at me for my carelessness. Partly, I was angry at the bank for catching me in an error. But mostly, I was scared that something bad would happen to me.

That was scary, but at least it was only a one time thing. My second husband, John, worked out of town and so the job of depositing his monthly paycheck into the bank always fell on my shoulders. This was long before the days of Internet banking and automatic deposits by employers. Because payday was always at the end of the month, I spent the last week of every month in sheer dread and terror. I had trouble sleeping and I felt nauseated all day long. I would try to talk my way out of the fear, but just picturing myself walking into the bank would send chills up my spine. I even tried to determine what I was actually afraid of and I think it came down to what follows.

My father had always said, "A man with no money, but no debts, is a successful man. A man with lots of money, and many debts, is a dismal failure." John and I did not have a lot of money and we had many debts, so, although he never said it, in my father's eyes we were even worse than dismal failures. I always thought that one day someone at the bank would figure that out and while I was standing in line at the teller's counter, I would be whisked off to wherever it was that they take people like us. I could not rationalize that we were doing nothing illegal or even wrong—we were in debt, and I never even considered that someday we would have our debts all paid off. I remember being very chatty to the teller so that she would be unable to concentrate; she would therefore not take notice of our "sins" and would not be able to turn us in. And, yes, according to my age, I was definitely an adult at that time!

I was afraid of the furnace coming on in the night. We were living in the huge house that John had built for me at South Cooking Lake, Alberta, in 1978, and for some mysterious reason that normal everyday sound was enough to put me into a full-blown panic attack every time. However, sometimes John would turn the furnace down so that it did not come on as often and then I would get scared because I thought it was malfunctioning.

I was terrified of driving in bad weather, but as we both worked in the same clinic in Sherwood Park, Alberta, I solved this by driving with my friend, Beth, for three entire winters. We got to know each other really well during those jaunts to and from work; essentially, that is when our friendship took form. Underneath, I always knew that I was with her because I was too terrified to be driving on my own, but as we both have some wonderful memories of those snowy, cold mornings in her big yellow car, I just pretended that I was there for our mutual fun of it.

I was paralyzed with fear by the thought of driving away from home in inclement weather, but I was equally afraid of leaving in beautiful weather because there was always the possibility that it would change before I got home. This actually happened the very first time I went to town after we had moved out to South Cooking Lake. It was a beautiful clear morning when I went into town, but when I returned late in the day, I found myself in the dark and in a major blizzard in which I could not see the road ahead of me. Because we had just moved to that area, I was not familiar with the twists and turns of the highway, and if it had not been for a semitrailer truck in front of me that flashed its hazard lights until we were out of worst of the blizzard, I do not think that I would have made it home that night. I have no idea how the driver of that truck knew that I was in as much emotional distress as I was, but somehow he did. I like to think that he was an angel dressed in trucker's clothing.

When I got home I just stood in the foyer of our brand new home and screamed that I hated living in the country; I hated my husband for building me this house; I hated him for going out of town to work; I hated him for leaving me alone to cope with this terror. That night, as I calmed myself down, I could feel Fear settling into me with a brand new kind of power and might. In essence, the frosty frigid weather outside did not hold a candle to the coldness that I could feel slowly creeping into my veins.

My fear of driving in bad weather was so notorious that if the Area Supervisor arrived at our lab and it was snowing, she would immediately come and tell me. If I had driven myself to work that day, she would instruct me to go home. She knew of my extreme fear and she realized that falling snow was only tolerable to me in daylight and by the time the lab closed it would be dark. She also knew that if I stayed at work, while knowing it was snowing outside, I would be useless, so she could not win either way. Needless to say, this supervisor was very happy when Beth drove me to work, because that eliminated the whole problem, which was really a pain in the proverbial butt for everyone who worked with me.

I was so afraid of being stuck in the snow in our 100 foot long driveway that I would get up numerous times in the night to see if it was snowing. If it was, I would go out in the dark and start shoveling. Sometimes I would be out there two or three times in one night if the snow was really coming down. I got claustrophobic just thinking about being in the house and unable to escape via the driveway due to snow coverage.

I was afraid of making commitments to anyone because I only did so when I was feeling good; more often than not, by the time it came to honor the commitment, I would have sunk into a dark, sad mood and would have to cancel. Knowing what I know now, I am more than a little bit sure that on some very deep level, I planned it that way. What a wonderful sabotage I had arranged for myself to subconsciously choose to be in a black mood just when it served me best. I will not say with absolute certainty that was the case, but it is definitely possible.

To succeed would be to take on a commitment that would be unbearable to handle. My way of handling this was to never stick with anything long enough to actually be seen as success-ful. I did well at everything that I ever attempted to do; hon-estly, and in complete modesty, I know that I am a talented and multiskilled woman. Over the years I excelled at macramé, ceramics, paper tole, quilting, sewing, knitting, painting figurines, jewelry making, photography, plus more. However, I did them obsessively until I lost interest, so noth-ing ever came of doing them. I would always spend a lot of money getting all the best supplies and then when I abruptly quit, the money spent was just one big waste. John always said that I would always get almost to the top of the mountain in anything I did, but as soon as I could see the summit, I would sit on my butt and slide back down to the bottom. I always fig-ured that if I succeeded at anything I would have to do it day in and day out for the rest of my life, and that would definite-ly be out of my realm of possibility. I did not know until recent-ly that no one likes to do the same thing over and over again forever. Balance was obviously something out of my range of understanding.

Here is one particularly strange dealing that I had with fear. When John built our house he intentionally put on wider overhangs than normal so that the house would be cooler in the summer. One day it was about 90 degrees outside, but inside it was quite chilly. I started putting on extra clothes to warm up, but no matter what I did I was still cold. Pretty soon, the cold air took on a life of its own and I felt like it would crush me. I ran outside, where I was shocked at how hot it was. However, I could not warm up, so I sat on the front step all bundled up and shaking as I tried to forget the feeling that the cold air in my house had actually felt like it was alive. I could not go into the house alone. I stayed outside until John came home many hours later from a golf tournament.

Then there were the fears that I can explain. I was terrified of being abandoned by people I love, especially the men in my life. I was paralyzed by the thought of making a fool of myself and I would move mountains to avoid being laughed at for anything, no matter how insignificant. But mostly I was afraid of being caught being the fraud that I knew myself to be. The child in me knew that she would not be loved if anyone saw her great sadness, so she built doors to hide behind. Sometimes the door was anything that would keep the fears at bay. For a number of years the door was her bedroom door, which she hid behind every chance she got because it was the only place where she could be herself. With her dad and later with her second husband, the door was a partition down the middle of her so that they could only see what she chose for them to see. And finally, the door became disguised as the cloak of depression. There, she was safe. There, she was warm and cozy. There, she was very comfortable. And there she stayed for many years.

FEAR

Somewhere deep inside of me
There's a little girl in tears.
She's afraid someone will hear her—
Merely one of many fears.
How can one so little
Be fearful of so much?
Is her fear the paralyzer
Or is it just a crutch?
Day after day, the panic grows
Within her tender breast.
She cries to God within her,
"Please, one hour of blissful rest."
The world out there is scary,
So hard, so cruel, so cold.
Little girls can make no choices,
They just do as they are told.
Sometimes she gets so tired
Just trying to keep ahead.
Fearing they'll discover her secret
Fills her little heart with dread.
To know what her Goliath is
Would make it possible to beat.
Faceless, nameless enemies
Are slow to fall in defeat.

Marilyn Avient

CHAPTER 2

When a child is as fearful as I was, he or she creates survival rules. We all have them, and after much investigating and soul-searching I believe that I know what some of mine are. Survival rules are created between the ages of 2 and 5, and while they may work well in childhood, they create havoc when carried over into adulthood.

As a small child, I looked out into the world to try to figure out how it operates. I took note of everything that I saw, heard, or felt and came to my own conclusions. A child takes the blame or credit for everything that happens in his or her world, so if the event felt good I would have said, "Gee, I'm wonderful! I'm such a good girl." Conversely, if the event was scary or just plain uncomfortable, I would have reacted as such: "I guess I'm really unlovable/stupid/ugly/unworthy. I can't let this happen again, so what do I need to change?" Children never blame anyone else for their painful experiences—they only blame themselves.

For instance, a 3-year-old boy and his mother are holding hands as they are walking in a shopping mall. The little boy trips on a shoelace and falls down on the hard concrete floor, skinning his knees. He begins to cry as he sees tiny droplets of red appear. The mother can have one of two extreme reactions.

The first is to stoop to comfort her son in his pain. She tells him she loves him and apologizes for walking so fast; then she kisses his knees all better. As soon as she does that, the boy jumps up and is ready to continue their walk. He holds his mom's hand, confident that he is loved and special. This incident will be forgotten within minutes.

The other reaction is to jerk her son to his feet so roughly that she almost pulls his arm out of its wee socket. She tells him to stop crying and quit being so clumsy. She tells him that he is just as stupid and ugly as his damned father. She starts walking again, dragging her sobbing child behind her. This young boy will not forget this incident and will set out immediately to change his ways. He knows he is stupid, clumsy, and ugly now and he will do anything he can to hide those facts from everyone around him for the rest of his life. Although it happened just one time, this incident, as seen from the innocence of a 3-year-old, is enough to cause the child to create survival rules. That sounds dramatic, but to the small child it truly is a matter of life and death. The child in the second scenario could possibly become a superbly groomed honor student who is a whiz on the basketball court (or he could be a skater or a great dancer). He does not ever want to experience that humiliation again and he has to make sure that no one guesses his secret.

We all have childhood survival rules in operation all of the time. It is not necessary to have the type of parent who would jerk your arm out of its socket in order to have these rules come into being. Even a well-adjusted parent can have a bad day and say something that is interpreted as unkind and unloving by the child. Even loving parents have their own emotional baggage and survival rules to deal with, so I think it is safe to say that they are doing the best they can with their own limited knowledge. Childhood survival rules are a fact of life, but their presence does not mean the child had bad parenting. They mean that he or she has suffered emotional pain but the intent, on the part of the person involved, is not important at the time. Only as an adult, when the child is doing some healing and retrospective work, does the intent of the parent come into play.

I have discovered three outstanding events in my childhood that contributed greatly to my collection of survival rules. The first one happened when I was only 18 months old while we were living in Dawson Creek, British Columbia, which is where I was born. On October 28, 1949, my maternal grandmother passed away in Alberta, so Mom had to go away for a week to attend the funeral, leaving my father to care for me and my two older sisters. From the time she left until the time she returned home, there was no communication between her and Dad because few people had phones in their homes in those days. Within hours of Mom's departure, my father had to rush me to hospital because I had come down with galloping pneumonia. For 48 hours the doctors were not sure if I would live. It would not have been unusual if I had died because, in that era, death from pneumonia was not only commonplace— it was almost expected. In a home where my mother was in charge of everything to do with house and children, my poor father must have almost gone out of his mind with worry as he tried to deal with this crisis alone.

When Mom came home, she immediately came to the hospital. When I saw her I apparently went crazy with excitement and happiness. I laughed, and cried, and hollered, and generally made an unacceptable fuss, which caused quite a stir with the hospital personnel. In 1949, you could not speak louder than a whisper in a hospital, and it was even required by law that you drive slowly and quietly past hospitals. I remember seeing signs that said, "QUIET. HOSPITAL ZONE"; thus, children were not allowed to play in the street or on the grounds surrounding a hospital. In light of that mentality, my excitement was received with disdain and my mother was escorted out and told to go home. Not only that, but she was banned from coming back to the hospital because they said that her effect on me could and would not be tolerated. For days she begged them to let me come home, so she could care for me herself. When I failed to make progress in the hospital, the doctor gave in and under Mom's care I was on the mend in no time.

For the rest of my life, I loved my mom best when I was not well. I remember being excited when I felt too sick to go to school because that is when my mom gave me the best attention. My mother was homemaker extraordinaire—she was on a mission to undo the wrongs and filth of her own childhood. She succeeded in every aspect except that she was so busy she never had time for me. In discussions with my mom she admitted that of all the children I was the one who was most alone merely because of my placement in the family—my sisters were in school and my brother had not been born yet. However, when I was sick that all changed. Only then did I get her undivided attention; only then did I feel really loved.

This incident also brought about a lifetime of homesickness. When I was growing up, it was senseless to even consider going away from home because I felt like I could die (a subconscious reliving of my experience with pneumonia). Needless to say, I missed out on a lot of fun. Girl Guide camp was fun, but I hated it because I missed Mom and home too much. In later years, I did not go into nursing because I would have had to live in a dormitory and I did not think that I could handle that.

When I got married to my first husband at 19, I was so lonely at first that it was physically painful. As recently as 1998 when I was 50 years old my second husband and I went to Arizona for two months. Believe it or not, I was homesick and the only person who could alleviate my sadness was my mother. That is when I realized that I would have to do some more delving into our relationship because it was inevitable that she was going to die and leave me one day. All of this pain originated in me because my grandmother innocently died before I was ready to be separated from my mother.

At this very young age, I learned much about fear. I learned that people leave and it is so scary when they go that it feels like the life has been sucked out of you. Some people say that emotion is symbolized by water or fluids (thus we cry when feeling emotional) and I find it interesting that pneumonia is the lungs filling up with fluid. In essence, I got so upset at her leaving that I almost drowned in my own fluids (emotions). I also realized that there are stiff penalties for being too boisterous with my emotions. I have always been very careful and very particular about where I choose to let my full emotions come out. I started to believe there were things to be afraid of in this world and, because I did not know what those things were, I decided to be afraid of everything. At a very young age, I took the saying "There is much to fear" as my personal truth and my most trusted words to live by.

Along a similar line, I was hospitalized when I was 7 years old, but this time it was to have my tonsils removed. In those days, tonsils were taken out on a whim and it seemed as though their removal could solve any health problem. If a person has his or her tonsils removed today (which is rare), he or she would perhaps be in hospital overnight, but probably would go home the same day. In 1955, I was kept in bed in hospital for ten days. I was so homesick that one night the nurses caught me literally trying to climb a wall—I was *that* delirious in my sadness. When my mother left after a visit with me, the last thing she saw every day was her daughter's body up against the glass partition screaming at her to come back. I can still feel the terror I felt at being left alone in that place.

Another event that brought about some survival rules happened when I was just over 2 years of age, not long after the pneumonia incident while we were still living in Dawson Creek. My father was in the army and we lived in army housing across the road from a huge field. This should have been an ideal place for the children of the area to play, but that was not the case because a coal mine was on the other side of the field. At that time there were few, if any, government agencies in place to protect the environment, so this was not a safe situation. There were no fences around the mine to keep children out and there were no filters in the mine to keep the coal dust from spewing everywhere, causing the field to be black with soot; it was thus an unsafe place to play.

I believe that I was a precocious little girl and a little thing like an unsafe blackened field beside a coal mine was not enough to stop me. I had a little male friend named Paddy and we went off to play in the field despite being told not to. Apparently we had come back covered in coal dust many times before the day of this incident.

Before I tell you the story of what happened that day, I would like to relate some pertinent information. First, this was 1950 and the common method for washing clothes was a wringer washing machine. Monday was wash day and generally it took all day to do little else but the washing and the ironing. Each load had to be put through the machine twice to be

Marilyn Avient

washed and rinsed; then it all had to be hung on the line to dry. When the line was full, Mom had to wait until that load dried before she could do any more. Because polyester was still a thing of the future, every piece of the laundry had to be ironed—even the towels and the sheets. Doing laundry was a huge job, to say the very least. I remember Mom bringing in rock-solid stiff sheets off the line in the winter that were so big and inflexible that she had trouble getting them through the doorway. I am sure that clothes covered in coal dust were not something that she relished adding to the already miserable job of doing the laundry.

Secondly, Mom had a rule. In her attempt to be a good and effective parent, she tried very hard to not make any threats that she was unable to carry out. Most of the time this was a good rule and most of the time it saved my siblings and me from getting any terrible punishments—except on that particular day. This story was a family joke for all of my life. Everybody saw it as funny and maybe it was. I thought it was funny too, up until 1995 when I told it to my favorite therapist, Dr. Radner. After he heard the story, he said, "That wasn't funny! That was abuse!" Here is the story.

One day, probably in sheer frustration because she had been formerly unsuccessful at keeping me away from the field, Mom apparently said, "Judy, if you come back today all black and sooty I'm going to . . . uh . . . hang you on the clothesline!" I can just picture her trying to think of something that would actually scare me enough to not only stay clean, but to stay away from the field. But I was 2 years old, and it would take more than that to scare me, so off I went to play with my friend Paddy. Little did I know it would be for the last time.

As you have probably guessed, Paddy and I came back a little later all black and sooty from playing where we had been told not to play. When Mom saw me, she probably felt quite distressed because she knew that she had to do what she had threatened if I was going to learn anything. That is when she got creative. She rigged up an old garter belt into a halter carrier and put me in it before swinging me out onto the line. The event caused quite a stir because no one had ever seen anything like this before. My sisters laughed. The neighbors laughed. I bet even Paddy laughed. The story goes that I laughed and then I cried and then I slept. Apparently I was left there for about three hours.

Everyone assumed the same little girl came off the line that went on, but they could not be more mistaken. Although I do not remember this event, I feel like I do because I have heard the story so often. However, what they did not tell me was that while I was hanging like an old shirt on that horrible clothesline, I probably created some rules of survival that would stay with me for the next 50 years. After all, this is not like the momentary sting of a spanking; this is humiliation and the pain of that takes a long time to wear off. Based on the way I lived my life after that, these are the rules that I believe I subconsciously made that day as I swung on that line:

Playing with boys is bad. (I never had a platonic male friend again until 1999.)

Getting dirty is really bad. (I have never done anything that involved getting dirty again.)

Authority figures are to be feared-that day Mom became an authority figure.

I must never make a fool of myself again. I feel bad when people laugh at me.

Be perfect. Perfect girls do not get humiliated.

Do not let anybody surprise you again. Stay ahead of everybody all the time.

Fun and spontaneity are not good. No more playing.

Of course, the little girl did not think that way, in those words, but based on how I have lived my life, these rules make sense. She probably just decided that she had to be a really good girl from that day on. She did stop playing with boys. She did stop playing with toys. She did stop getting dirty. She did stop disobeying. I think that life took on very serious overtones for the little girl who was me. I was very much of a loner as a child and to this day I do not like doing anything silly. Until I was about 40 years old I never even played cards because I did not like games; I did not trust the concept of having fun. I never liked cartoons because they were too silly. I did not like nursery rhymes or stories of fantasy, and on that I have never wavered to this day. To me an enjoyable story is one that is true to life and full of victory of the spirit; if it does not wring some tears out of me then it is just a waste of my time. I know that the child in me was seriously injured that day and no one meant to do it. Mom never had to really punish me for anything ever again because from that day on, I was a good girl— a serious, sad, responsible good girl.

I must add that I believe the story had to be kept alive for all those years for a very good reason. I was too young to remember it, but I needed to be continually told about it so that I could discover in 1995 what effect that day had on my life. From the day I told the therapist about it, my stint on the clothesline was amazingly never mentioned by my family again. Until now, I have never discussed my findings with any of them. They told it until I did not need to hear it anymore. The Universe has just the most intriguing way of handling things!

My next set of survival rules were provided by my favorite person on the planet: my father. Because Dad was in the army, our family moved around a lot—Mom became an expert packer during our more than 20 moves over the years. Sometimes, however, Dad got orders to go places where there were no provisions for families, so he had to go alone. As hard as it was to constantly pack up and move, the times when Dad went off for long stretches by himself were even harder. One such lone posting happened in the fall of 1952 when I was 4 years old.

I woke up one morning and Dad was gone. Mom told me that he had gone overseas (which was very far away) and he would not be back for a year. *I was to find out much later that he had taken part in the Canadian army's mission to clean up Holland after its occupation by the Nazis during World War II.* I doubt that I had any concept of how long a year was, but I knew it must be very long because everyone was sad. I have a suspicion that the day before he left, I must have been in one of my sad moods, because I remember deciding that it was my fault he had left. If he came back, I vowed that I would never let him see me sad again. Now, as an adult, I know this reasoning is ridiculous, but to that 4-year-old it made perfect sense.

That was a very lonely time for me. My sisters, Sharon and Barbara, who were 7 and 5 years older than me, were in school all day, leaving me all by myself. I remember wanting to go to school so bad that I would take some books and walk around outside with them pretending that I was walking to school like my sisters.

During the year when Dad was gone, Mom was very sad because not only did she have total responsibility for everything to do with our lives, but she missed her husband and was pregnant with my brother, David. Mom had even less time for me then because she was busy as well as sad. When David was born in April of 1953, I lost Mom all over again because she now had a wee baby to care for. Ironically, as was my pattern, when I woke up the day that he was born, Mom was gone. The lady who was going to sit with us was there and told me that Mom had gone to the hospital in the night. I was very anxious; now both my parents were gone! Was she coming back? Did I do something wrong that made her leave? When she came home a week later, she was carrying a baby; I remember having a stomachache and taking a long time to warm up to my brother because he made Mom leave me.

When Dad left without saying good-bye and, in essence, stealing off in the middle of the night, I decided that was what men do. If I was going to prevent that from happening again, I would have to be the best daughter and make his life so wonderful that he would never want to leave ever again. I spent a lot of time in our living room listening to songs on the radio and quietly playing by myself—my favorite pastime was to pretend that all the books on the shelves were in a library and I was the librarian. I was a very old, very lonely little girl.

Somehow I made it through that year that felt like forever—when you think about it, by the time he got back my dad was absent—that time—for 20% of my life. I remember well the night that Dad arrived home because I spent the day doubled over with stomach pain. As the evening drew closer, the pain became worse: partly from overwhelming excitement and partly because I knew from that day forward I would have to be the best girl in the world so that my dad would not leave me again. The responsibility was already lying heavy upon me. That same stomach pain over the years would return whenever I was feeling responsible for keeping our family happy and together. To me, stomach pain represented fear and futility!

My memory of the night that my dad returned from

Holland looked like this. I vividly remember standing on the wooden platform at the train station, waiting for the sound of the whistle signaling the arrival of the train carrying the person I loved the most in the world back to me. When the train arrived it was so packed with soldiers that some of them had to stand. From an observer's point of view, the first car that pulled into the station looked like it was literally stuffed with soldiers all anxious to see their loved ones once more. I saw him looking expectantly out the window; when he saw me, he rushed out, picked me up, and swung me around before hugging me soundly. I felt happy. I felt complete. I felt safe for the first time in a year.

In about 1990 I was talking to Mom about that day and for some reason I mentioned the wooden platform. She looked at me oddly and told me that the platform was very large and made of concrete. I conceded that maybe I was wrong on that but when I mentioned the train being packed with soldiers, she said, "There were only two soldiers on that train and one of them was your dad. It was such an event to have a soldier coming home in 1953 that a reporter from the *Edmonton Journal* took our picture for the news the next day." I was absolutely puzzled by her revelation because no matter what she said, my memory of that night was crystal clear. In fact, I was not only confused, I was very sad and I had a feeling of loss.

Not long after the talk with Mom, I was out for a walk and, without provocation, I said right out loud, "My dad was not my first soldier to come home by train." I stopped walking and knew that I had just hit something big. When I discussed it with Dr. Radner, he said that similar memories from different lifetimes occasionally overlap and become confused with one another. Because I know I have lived many lifetimes before this one, his information did not cause me any undue stress at all; in fact, it made me feel very relieved. Mom's version was right, but so was mine. I had met a train on a wooden platform in another place at another time and the soldier in that memory did pick me up and swing me around. In both scenarios I had been very lonesome and very afraid because the soldier in my life had left me for a long period of time.

Once my dad was back, my work began in earnest; he had no idea that, by not saying good-bye on just one night when I was 4 years old, he would impact my life for the next half of a century. He did it because he could not bear to see me sad at his leaving, but in retrospect a little sadness that night would have been merciful compared to the ongoing pain and fears that ultimately led to one fateful day in adulthood.

CHAPTER 3

March 29, 1984, was the day that divided my life into two parts. Whenever I remember any part of my life, it is always classified as to whether it happened before or after that date. On that day, I collapsed physically, mentally, emotionally, and spiritually. In the morning I was working as usual in the lab in Sherwood Park; by late afternoon I was a patient on the psychiatric ward of the old Edmonton General Hospital. To everyone else it looked like it should have been the worst day of my life, but to me it was one of the best. It was the day I finally got off the inner runaway roller coaster that had been my life and had the chance to just bow out for a while. Unbeknown to me at the time, it was the beginning of a spiritual quest that continues to this day. All the childhood experiences and all the rules that I made to help me cope with my life were the beginning of that collapse.

Before I reached the ripe old age of 6, I had already figured out what I had to do to survive peaceably in my world. In actuality, I had probably already decided what I could and could not do with my life just by the lessons I had already learned. I had come to conclusions that I saw as being correct well into my adult life and some of them even took me into the years of my husband's retirement. The power of a small child is phenomenal considering what those rules do to us even when we think of ourselves as "all grown up."

I had decided (based on the actions of the influential adults in my life) that in order to be loved, I had to take care of everybody around me. Not only did I need to be needed; I needed to be indispensable. I learned that men leave me when I am sad, so I decided to pamper and dote on them in order to stop that from happening. I learned that when people I love leave me, it is so scary, and so painful, that to die would be merciful. I learned that saying good-bye is a horrible experience that should be avoided at all costs.

The fears that stopped me every time I turned around started before my long-term memory even began. I have known fear every day of my life. To cover up the fears and make sure that no one knew about my unworthiness, I had to find coping methods and the first one of these was perfectionism.

There are perfectionists—and then there are perfectionists. I am not the variety that cannot tolerate a speck of dust or a dish out of place; rather, I grew up thinking I had to be perfect in my relationships. There seemed nothing unnatural about expecting to be the perfect wife, the perfect mother, the perfect daughter, the perfect sibling, the perfect student, the perfect friend, the perfect employee, and even the perfect citizen of the world. For a person who had such grave concerns about people laughing at her or generally making a fool of herself, I was certainly setting myself up for doing just that when I aspired to be faultless in all the relationships of my life.

As I write this, I am doing some soul-searching and I am sad to admit that one of those *perfect* relationships was an outright lie! I hear menacing laughter that is very loud, very accusatory, and very well deserved when I think about my relationship with my sons for the first 18 years of their lives. As you will see,

I foolishly took their love for granted and so, in their presence, I exposed all my fears and insecurities, placing them firmly on their young and undeserving shoulders. However, the man who could have relieved me of some of my fears was the person I foolishly trusted the *least* in my world.

I thought that if I were the perfect wife, my second husband John would never leave me as my father had done when he crept off in the night for the year-long posting to Europe. I did everything in my power to make myself so necessary to John that he would stick around simply because he could not function without me. Full-scale pampering of my husband was possible because he worked out of town 80% of the time, thus giving me much reprieve. I had many days all to myself so when he was around it was no hardship to dote on him.

For the first nine years of our marriage, he never packed one suitcase, even though he went out of town every week. I decided early on that this was a way I could become indispensable to him, and I milked it for all I was worth. Every week, I ironed and folded his shirts and pants with care and made sure he had just the right amounts of everything he could possibly need for the time he was gone. I usually included a love note and a treat of some sort, and I assumed he loved how I did all these things for him.

However, one day, about a month before my breakdown, John came to me with a request. He had a shirt in his hand and he looked very serious. Knowing how sensitive I was to criticism, he did choose his words carefully, but to no avail. He said that he wondered if I would mind folding his shirts a different way than I had been doing. He showed me how my method left a crease and then proceeded to show me the way he would like me to fold them. I watched, took it all in, and nodded in agreement, but inside I shriveled with humiliation.

Here was a task that I did because I wanted to be needed by him, and here he was, telling me that I had been doing that task improperly for nine years. And then he added salt to my wound by showing me that *he* knew a better way to do it. Not only was I not perfect, but he made me feel like a fool, which broke one of my cardinal rules of childhood. He was perfectly capable of packing a suitcase; he had just shown me that he did not need me at all. I felt like he was *letting* me do it, but he did not *need* me to do it. My reaction was totally out of proportion, but that is how I always responded to criticism because, according to my rules, there should not have been any. Perfect people doing perfect things do not get criticized. This incident was so small that it should have been forgotten immediately, but instead it became so big and so important that it is being written about more than 20 years later. I no longer wanted to pack his suitcases and I hated that he actually still expected me to do this job. This one little reasonable request brought the day of my breakdown much, much closer.

People-pleasing was another trick that I used to cover up my inadequacies, my philosophy being, that if they are pleased with me, they will love me. However, that did not account for the fact that according to my rules, I had to please the whole world—even those who did not know me. I have walked into a store, and if the clerk looked irritated or grumpy, I would wonder what I had done to cause this. If my teachers were in a bad mood when I was in school, I would spend the day trying to make them smile. I was sure that if my boss was having a bad day, then I was responsible and I had to work extra hard to make up for it. I honestly thought that I would be fired by one particular boss who was grumpy more often than not; it made perfect sense to me to assume that it was entirely my fault. I have often thought that for a girl with low self-esteem, I sure had a big ego if I thought I could affect that many people to such an extreme.

One of the follies of people-pleasing is that one often *gives to get* instead of *giving to give*. I used to be the world's greatest gift giver, but mostly for the wrong reasons. On Christmas Day in 1982, fifteen people were at my home for dinner including my immediate family. I had bought presents for everyone and had sorted the wrapped packages into piles for each person in the den. My sons and husband always received about 30 gifts each from me, but there were plenty for everyone else as well. In fact, I counted over 300 gifts in the den on Christmas Eve when I went in to check that I had enough. Well, as silly as that sounds, my older son, Sean, came in and found me sobbing my heart out because I did not see enough presents—and I really did not! I told him that I had to go to town to do some more shopping, but somehow he calmed me down and talked me into going back to the kitchen to continue making our Christmas Eve dinner. Even with a dozen presents per person (besides my kids and my husband), I did not think that was enough to make them love me. I went back to the kitchen, but I sure was worried. Years later, my friend, Gail, who was there that day told me that she was always embarrassed by the vast numbers of gifts she received from me each year. That really surprised me because I thought it was expected of me; I thought she would love me for it. To me the concept was easy: the more gifts I give, the more love I will get.

People-pleasing went to another point of ridiculousness for me. We lived in the country and part of the highway into the city was divided, but part of it was only two lanes, so I had to contend with two-way traffic. I was always under pressure on the two-way section because if any other driver chose to overtake me, I took it personally, thinking that person was displeased with me. One day, I remember pulling over to the side of the road and crying because someone had overtaken me. I did not give any credence to the suggestion that maybe that person was driving too fast or was hurrying because of an emergency; all I knew was that he or she was mad at me and I was sick about it. This kind of thinking, day after day, was very wearing.

Because my mother surprised me the day that she hung me on the line, I knew that I could never let that happen again. I made a rule that I had to be ten steps ahead of everyone, and not just sometimes, but every single day of my life. That is an exhaustive chore to say the least. Every day I made myself figure out what *everyone* around me would need in the next 24 hours. Believe it or not, I actually became quite adept at it.

As mentioned earlier, I was working in a medical laboratory at the time of my breakdown. Even though I was the head technologist of our particular lab, I had a supervisor who was in charge of all the labs in the area. Every day I went into work early and made a point of making sure everything was done so that there was nothing that she could call me on. One day, I remember her casually saying, "Judy, I wonder if you would mind doing [some small task] for me." It was said kindly and lightly, but I did not take it that way. In my mind, I heard her saying, "Judy, you stupid girl, why didn't you know that I would need this [small task] done today? You're a failure and if you keep this up you'll be fired." I did what she asked, but I beat myself up very badly for not knowing ahead of time what she would want.

I had another habit that was a type of coping skill, but it hindered more than helped me get through life. As part of my responsibility for keeping the whole world happy, I foolishly decided that I could take away pain from those around me. When my father died, I honestly and truly thought that I could take my mother's grief and feel it *for* her. Then *she* could be happy. This was not done whimsically or lightly; it was done consciously and with childlike innocence, truly believing that I could effectively put an end to another person's suffering. However, even if this task were possible to do, it was not done for the right reasons. I thought the pain of my mother's suffering was more tolerable for me to experience than how I would feel seeing her looking sad and unhappy. Her continued unhappiness made me afraid, because that meant I was failing at keeping those around me happy in hope that they would stay.

In 1983, the 18-year-old son of one of my co-workers was killed in a motor vehicle accident. We spent a lot of time talking about her grief. One day, I realized that I was grieving for this boy as though he were my own. Even when she was not in my presence I was suffering the loss of *my* child. After a while, I was not sad for her loss, I became sad for mine. March 29, 1984, was drawing closer.

Also in 1983, Mary, another friend from work, who had been adopted as a baby, asked me to write the story of her long but ultimately successful quest to find her birth mother. I started the story with great enthusiasm, even interviewing all the people from both her adoptive and her biological families. Her newly found family lived near Vancouver, British Columbia, so I flew there from Alberta to spend a few days talking to her birth mother and all her new brothers and sisters. I had many pages of factual notes to use, but when I got home I started writing the story from "memory" as though *I* was the birth mother, adding details that came from *me* and not from *her*. Eventually, her pain became my pain and I hurt so badly that I was unable to finish the story. This was just one more tidbit of distress that led to my breakdown, which was fast approaching.

Ironically, Mary had been born in the same hospital where I later became a patient. The psychiatric ward was in the new section, but one day I decided to go for a long walk and went to the old part of the hospital and walked the corridors. When I got to the old maternity ward, I had to immediately go back to my room, because the flood of feelings that came over me as *I remembered the day the baby I gave up for adoption was born* was just too much to bear. The story remains unfinished to this day.

CHAPTER 4

Now let's go back a few years. My first marriage was one of those double-edged swords: one side of it was love and the other side was poison. My first husband Dan and I had started dating in 1964 when I met him walking down the street while a friend and I were walking home from the shopping center. He and his buddy sidled up beside us and started talking. Dan was a very nice-looking guy who always wore dress pants and often a tie with his shirt; in all the years I have known him I never saw him in a pair of blue jeans. As we walked and talked he asked me for my phone number and, of course, being the well-brought up girl that I was, I told him that I could not possibly give it to him. However, being a smooth talker, Dan told me that he would tell me his and I guess that was supposed to make it all right. Lo and behold, something very interesting happened—our phone numbers had the exact same figures, but in different sequences. (My number was 455-0872 and his was 455-7082.) I did not give him my exact number, but I told him that it was the same as his—only different; for some reason that made me feel like I could go home with my virginity intact, so to speak. I guess the next day Dan tried many variations of his phone number until he finally found the right one. We went out that night to see the movie, *The Pink Panther*, and that was the beginning of a very loving but tumultuous relationship.

I was given a clue very early on in our "romance" that things were not the way I wanted them to be. I probably did not want to pay attention because it would be one of those things that would make one of my greatest fears come true— that I was unlovable! Dan told me very soon after our first date that he had really wanted to meet my friend when he came up behind us that night. And after he told me that, he did not add, "But I am really glad that you are the one that I called." Instead of remarking on it like I should have, I just let it be.

When I met him, Dan was going to preseminary college instead of going to public high school. He was in grade 10 and I was in grade 11. He stayed in a dorm at the college and was only allowed "out" for one weekend every month. We met in August so for one full school year, I waited for those very rare weekends when I would get to see him again. When he came home we had a lot of fun and were together every possible minute of the weekend. We both talked about how much fun we would have when the summer finally came.

The school year ended at the end of June and I was so excited to spend the summer with Dan that I could hardly see straight. And then, life got in the way. The week before he finished for the year, his big brother said that he had bought a fast food place in a small town in Alberta; he told Dan that he wanted him to run it for the summer. As soon as the school doors opened to let the students out for the summer, his parents and I drove him to his new job. We hugged good-bye and Dan said that he would be home for a weekend very soon. I was devastated! I seemed to be spending all my time wishing my life away as I waited for those rare weekends with my boyfriend to arrive.

The long-awaited Friday night finally came to pass, and Dan picked me up to go to a dance at the local community hall where our favorite band was playing. He seemed a little more reserved than I would have expected, but I put it down to him being tired after working so many days in a row. We made it through the dance with less magic than I had imagined there would be, and before we were even out the door of the hall, Dan broke it to me. He told me that he had met a girl that he wanted to be with more than he wanted to be with me. I could not believe what I was hearing and when I grabbed his arm to plead with him to not leave me, Dan pulled away and I actually ripped the sleeve right off of his jacket. I was crying so hard that he almost had to carry me home; luckily the hall was only a couple of blocks from my home.

My father always waited up until all of us kids were home from our evening activities. One day I asked him why he did that when none of the other parents did. He told me, "I want to make sure that you are as happy when you come home as you were when you went out." That night I finally knew exactly what he meant. I knew he would be waiting for me, which on one hand was very comforting, but on the other, I actually had the audacity to worry that he would be mad at Dan for hurting me. I even tried to fake it when I walked into the house, but my dad had little trouble not missing the fact that my mascara was running down my face and, more obviously, Dan was minus one sleeve. Dad went outside and talked to Dan, then he came in and held me until I stopped crying.

My world absolutely came to a screaming halt. I had spent the past year waiting for that one weekend per month when I would feel important to someone besides my parents. All my friends had steady boyfriends and Dan made me feel like I was one of the "in girls." I was certainly not one of them, but I felt like I was when I was with him. I knew when Dan left me for that girl that I would never have a boyfriend again because he had only proved once more what I had always known—I was unlovable and I was not pretty enough to be anybody's girlfriend. I actually stayed in bed for a few days, then Mom made me get off my butt and get back to the land of the living. Mom and Dad would have had Dan lynched if they had had any say in the matter.

I went back to my job at Eaton's and every other week or so Dan's mother would just happen to come by. She told me that she did not really like his new girlfriend, emphasizing that she certainly did not like him bringing her home with him for weekends. I hated hearing the news about him, and yet I could not get enough. Finally, one day, she gave me some good news.

Dan was back in town to start school in September and he was suddenly unattached. She innocently mentioned that she knew he would be home that night if I wanted to just drop by. Having not one ounce of pride in me, I did just that. Can you imagine anything so pathetic? I can only imagine what he thought of me, but lo and behold, we talked and started going out again. By Christmas, Dan had given me a lovely black diamond ring. I thought my world was perfect and beautifully tied up in a big red, unbreakable bow.

For the next three years we dated and once in a while we talked about marriage. I was in training to be a medical lab technician and Dan was finishing grade 12, now at a public high school. Somewhere in that year when we were still ridiculously young, I decided that if Dan was not going to ask me to marry him, then I would make it happen on my own. Once more, I did something that, upon looking back, I cannot believe how little self-esteem I had because I just jumped right in and did it. I talked to my parents and when I finally had them convinced it was a good thing to do, I called Dan and told him that we could get married. Actually, if I remember correctly, my father's words were, "I don't think it is the right thing because you are too young, but you are probably going to go ahead and do it anyway, so I will give you my blessing." Dan talked to his parents and we set a date: January 6, 1968.

The wedding day came and went. Everything seemed like a dream come true—at least it did to me. Our first son, Sean, was born March 29, 1969, and because Dan was going to college, I had to go back to work when my baby was only three weeks old. In those days there was no such thing as paid maternity leave. I was earning the whopping sum of $429 per month at my first job, which was in a privately owned lab in downtown Edmonton. With all this cash at our disposal we thought we were in the land of the rich and famous. In 1969, that was a good wage—for a woman!

One weekend, after he finished his schooling, Dan went to a Catholic retreat house to get some perspective about his difficulty handling his nerves in regard to his new sales job. I was glad that he would have some time to relax and calm down, but I missed him dreadfully. When he came home, I had a lovely supper ready for him and was just bubbling with happiness on having him home. I will never know why he had to tell me, but when I asked why he was so quiet, he said that he had fallen for one of the nuns at the retreat house. He knew that he could never have her, but he would never forget her either. There can be no explanation as to why he thought that I should know about this crush of his except that he wanted to hurt me. It worked beautifully—that was the first obvious crack in the foundation of our marriage.

In the 1970s it was still not "cool" to have any kind of mental illness—and that includes depression. If someone was depressed they were said to be sad, or melancholy, or just downright ungrateful for the good life they had. No one used the word *depressed* to mean anything more than "I am so depressed—that dress I wanted was not there when I went back to buy it!"

I had no idea that I was [mentally] ill because I had been the same way all my life. I could be feeling really good and flirty and funny one day, and sucking slough water the next. That was the way I had always been so I did not see it as being abnormal. I did spend a lot of time in our bedroom, lying down and crying. I did a lot of deep sighing and generally just gave off an air of sadness. Dan said he was sick and tired of me being so down all the time and, of course, that scared me because I figured he would soon be gone. When we did split, it was initiated by me. Looking back, I truly think that I felt it would be better if I did the leaving instead of being left.

Before that happened our second son, Jason, was born on November 17, 1970. That was the best thing that happened during that period. The 1970s were notorious for partying, drinking, drugging, and free love. Dan and I held or attended a party every Saturday night and every week I flirted with every man in the room; I could have had an affair with almost any of them. The room could be lit up with the amount of electricity that was passing between the men and the women at the parties—and I do not mean between husbands and wives. As for myself, I ended up having a few affairs during those first years of our marriage—definitely not a good start for any husband and wife team! I felt the most alive when I was flirting and dancing and making a spectacle of myself, especially in front of men who belonged to other women.

In 1972, Dan was transferred through his work to a lovely city in British Columbia. At first everything went well and even at a time of low employment I was able to land a job in the lab in the local hospital. My last affair before Dan and I separated was with a doctor who had done jaw surgery on me. I was born with an off-centered lower jaw that I was very self-conscious about and I thought that fixing it would solve all my problems. As soon as my mouth healed, this doctor told me that he wanted to have an affair with me. I was so flattered. I had immediate proof of what a straight jaw can do for you!

This doctor's wealth and his position in life totally blew me away—to heck with the fact that he broke all the rules of medical ethics when he seduced me, his patient. He was married. I had even met his wife when she came through the hospital lab for tests. As a testimony to the morals of this outstanding citizen, he was with me the night one of his children was born! I felt very sorry for his wife because I knew that I was just one of many, but that was no justification for my behavior. I told Dan that I was seeing this other man—hoping that he would beg me to end it—he did not—but that did not break us up because he, too, had found someone else. We stayed together for a while, each going our own way and seeing other people like we were just roommates instead of a married couple.

Finally, I could not tolerate our horrible, sick, dishonest marriage anymore, so I told him that we had to split up. I took the boys and moved back to Edmonton. It was obvious that we still cared for each other because Dan and I talked and cried together for many hours the night before we parted. I know that his heart was breaking over losing his sons and I was crying over what might have been. We did love each other, but that did not seem to be enough. Dan was a good man and I was a good woman, but we were not good for each other. Like I said, one edge of the sword was love and the other was poison.

After we split up, Dan's mother told me that he had not loved me when we got married and that he had only gone through with the wedding because he did not want to hurt me.

She probably should not have told me that, but I think she wanted me to get on with my life once the decision was made to part. Dan and I were divorced on October 28, 1974, only five short years after our wedding.

CHAPTER 5

The doctor with the unscrupulous morals did give me one small piece of wisdom. He told me to be aware because the worst reason to return to a marriage is loneliness. He went on to tell me that the realization of being alone is like quicksand: once you fall into it, you sink fast and, in desperation, you grab for anything—even a marriage that was not working.

Dan and I went through that stage, but the conditions he put on my returning were just too unbearable and, equally, ridiculous. He was going to dictate where I could live, if I could work, what groups I could join, and whether I could have a car or not. He wanted me back for the wrong reasons, so we stayed apart and carried on with the divorce proceedings.

In 1974, the divorce laws were different. You could only get divorced for certain acceptable reasons, such as adultery, desertion, or abuse, and you did not even need a lawyer. Dan and I used the same lawyer and *we* told *him* what each of us would get. I got the furniture, half the dishes, and $25 per month per child! I signed away all rights to ever getting any alimony; obviously my people-pleasing skills were honed and in perfect working order!

Once I got over the shock of being single again, I started to have one heck of a good time. During my first year back in Edmonton, I worked in three different labs, then went to the best job on earth—customer service representative at a hospital supply company. This was a wild and crazy group; fun times were just part of the job. In fact, at my job interview, the male boss and I mostly talked about our favorite nightspots. When I sounded like I knew what I was talking about on the subject, he hired me. Just to follow the mandatory hiring criteria to a small degree, I had to pass an aptitude test that basically told him that I was living, breathing, and had an IQ higher than that of an ant.

After I had been on the job for a while I remember this same boss interviewing a girl who wanted to be hired as a typist. After their talk in the office, the boss told her that perhaps she should take a typing test. She looked at him and said, "I don't type." He shrugged his shoulders and said, "Maybe you'll learn. See you on Monday." He really was not a dumb man; his idea of what made a good employee was just a wee bit different than that of most people in management! Maybe this boss was smarter than we think; in the two years after I was hired the staff turnover was *zero*. We had a lot of fun. To his good fortune, I was great at my job!

We went out as a group once a week at least and, for the most part, there was a lot of flirting, but usually just harmless fun. I have never laughed so much in my life as I did with that group. Just to give you a hint as to the fun we had, I will tell you a story.

One night, there were about 10 of us out for dinner at a hotel in downtown Edmonton. Doreen and I were the only girls in the group. There were two salesmen in from out of town—I will call them Bob and Len. They were with different companies, but seemed to always be in town at the same time. After coinciding with each other a number of times, Bob and Len decided that it would save them money if they shared a hotel room. Believe me, they were as different as broccoli and peas—perhaps that is why they got along. On that particular night, Bob was out partying with us and Len was in their room because he always went to bed by 10 pm—we thought that he was dull and he thought that we were morons! Around 11 pm we were talking about Len going to bed so early and how he thought we were such a wild bunch.

So we came up with a plan. Bob let us into their room and we all snuck quietly over to his bed and the 10 of us piled in. How we did it without waking up Len is beyond me! When we were all in the bed and looking like we were in the midst of an orgy, Bob woke Len up. (In case you are wondering, we had all our clothes on!) When he saw us all in the bed he almost had a coronary—which would not have been much fun—and he pulled the blankets up over his head in disgust because he thought that we were all in the nude. We laughed until we could laugh no more, then we got out of the bed and went home. Harmless and stupid fun; nonetheless, I will remember that crazy job and all those fun people to the end of my days.

That was not the only fun that I took part in. I was out just about every night of the week. The two who suffered from this were my two sons, Sean and Jason. Every night at 8 pm I would put them to bed, the babysitter would arrive, and I would leave for another evening of fun. To put it nicely, I was very promiscuous. One day, I counted the number of men I had slept with during that 18-month period and all I will say is that I was very lucky to come out of that dismal part of my life with a clean bill of health. I was trying to feel important and loved by someone, even if it was only for a few minutes every night. I would not let myself think I was being used by these guys because I wanted to believe they really did care. I neglected my children; I disrespected my body and my soul; and when I was not out playing, I spent my time feeling guilty and shameful.

Every morning I would say that I would not go out again, but every night a mere phone call from a friend was enough to have me out until the wee small hours of the morning. I thought because I waited for my children to go to bed before I went out that I truly was that perfect mother that I aspired to be. I never even gave one bit of a thought to the fact that if my sons woke up in the night all they would see would be the face of the babysitter, but never their mom's. How selfish could I be leaving these two little people who were trying to cope with the loss of their father from their everyday lives? When it came to growing up, my kids were way ahead of me.

CHAPTER 6

In the midst of all my "living on the edge," the day came to officially divorce Dan. It was a day worth remembering and I mean that in the nicest way. On October 28, 1974, I drove over to my in-laws house to pick up Dan because we were driving to divorce court together. I guess you might say that we had our last date that day. We were doing this thing in such a civilized manner that, as mentioned earlier, we even shared a lawyer. Neither of us was contesting anything, so it would have been reckless of us to have separate lawyers, each of which needed to be paid.

I remember my mother-in-law not knowing what to say to me that day, which was very unusual because we had become very close since I moved back to Edmonton with Sean and Jason. I think she would have had more understanding and more to say if we had been handling this event with a little more animosity. But no, that was not the case. We had a lovely chat on the way to the courthouse. Dan asked me if I was sure I could take care of the boys. I was shocked at the question. I told him that I would not be doing this if there was any chance I would lose them. For a minute I was scared that he was going to fight me for them, but thankfully he was not.

When we got to the courthouse we had to take a number and wait our turn. Finally, after listening to the troubles of a few other couples, our names were called. I remember going into a state of unreality. All of a sudden I felt this could not be happening to me and I was terrified, but somehow I managed to get through my part of the ordeal with little trouble. The judge wanted me to ask for more money, but I told him that the amount agreed upon was just fine. He finally let me go and sit down. While Dan was on the stand, I realized that I was soon to be all alone, fending to make a life for me and our sons. I quietly prayed that the world be a kindly place for all of us to live in.

When the deed was done and the papers signed, we left the courtroom together. On the way back to his parents' place, Dan asked me if I would like to have a drink with him, to *celebrate* in a manner of speaking, and I agreed. We chose to go to the lounge that was on the corner where we had met ten years earlier. We sat in the semidarkness of the Sahara Lounge and cried in our drinks along with all the other poor souls who spent their afternoons hiding in those shadows. We were both overcome with a sadness that was almost unbearable, but bear it we must, because we both knew that we had messed up our lives and the lives of our children in a big way.

Just as we got our emotions somewhat under control, Dan's brother arrived proclaiming that he did not have a gift because he had never been to a divorce party before. I cannot even remember how he knew that we were there, but then there were three of us to commiserate. I did not want the afternoon to end, because when it did I knew that they would be going in one direction and I would be going in the other. I also knew that we would never share a table like this again. We were not good for one another, but we were comfortable together. We knew what to expect from one another and at that moment I think we both wished that we could forget what had just happened and go home to try again. On the emotional level, that may have been true, but intellectually we both knew that it was over. Too many hurts. Too many broken dreams. Too many lies. Too many tears. Too late to be good for each other ever again.

I finally stood up and said we had to get the inevitable over with. I kissed Dan good-bye. As we held each other for the last time, we cried again. I think both of us wondered why this was so necessary if we were both hurting so much. The moment passed. I turned and walked outside into the light. I took a deep breath and knew that I would be OK . . . someday, but not that day.

For the next two weeks, I put myself into a forced time of mourning. Looking back, I am quite amazed I had the foresight to know I had better get some of these tears out or else I would never heal. Dan and I may not have been good for each other, but we did the world some good by creating Sean and Jason, the only two boys who would one day be strong enough to handle the Hell that I would put them through.

As it turned out, Dan and I both made new lives with new people and, together, we celebrated all of the major events of our boys' lives with class and dignity. Not once did our sons ever have to be careful what to say about the other parent because we honestly respected one another, then and now. Dan and I made a shambles of our marriage but we sure were good at being divorced. Let it be known that I have no regrets whatsoever.

CHAPTER 7

I now need to tell you about a very special girl in my life. Her name was Lulubelle.

Lulubelle was a phenomenon that had no medical explanation. I am more than positive that few, if any, of the psychiatrists or nurses ever believed she was anything more than a figment of my overactive imagination. Because I knew when I was "her," and knew when I was "me," I was told that I was definitely not a multiple personality. They tried putting a few labels on me, but none of them fit, so I knew they did not know what was wrong with me, if there was anything wrong at all. To me, nothing was wrong; it was just as it always was!

Lulubelle was not named until 1984 when I was in hospital, but it is convenient to call her that in telling you about her early years so that I can differentiate "her" from "me." As a child I remember seeing a girl who looked exactly like me sitting with my dad in the living room while I stood in the hallway watching them. He was laughing. She was literally charming him and even flirting with him in a childlike way. I was amazed and equally distressed at how she looked so at ease and so in her element as she entertained him. I hated her because he looked completely enchanted, so obviously he loved her more than he loved me. I went to my room and cried. I knew she was the other side of me, but I thought everyone separated like that, so did not think anything of it. I just accepted that I hated the other girl, who was also me.

In the midst of all my traits, there were some that did not fit in; these were the ones that belonged to Lulubelle. Every once in a while, I would feel my heart racing, my pulse beating like I was going to explode, and all of a sudden I knew I was alive. Everyone around me also knew something different was happening and soon the show would begin. I was like a stand-up comedian who was having a great night and would come up with brilliance that was quite out of character for me. In that state, I could do *anything*. I always knew when "she" was around because before long I would have a kind of stomachache reserved for that situation only. No matter. When I was as high as I could get, I would never let a little pain stop me—not when I was flying!

If other people were around I would entertain them and make promises I could never keep in a million years. I made many to myself in that state, but it just meant that later I would have a lot of canceling to do or I would have to go back on many of the things I had said. Without exception, I always hated myself after one of those episodes.

If I was alone, I would go out and buy things I did not need, or start crafts for which I would have to buy tons of supplies, because I was sure I would be doing that craft for the rest of my life. One time I bought 40 balls of macramé yarn and only used 6 of them before I came down from my "high."

One day, at South Cooking, on one of my days off from work at the lab in Sherwood Park, Lulubelle showed up and we had nothing to do, so we decided to apply for a job—one I had no intention of doing. I did not want to *have* the job; I just wanted to *get* the job. I got a hold of the newspaper and looked for the job I was most unlikely to get. I found one for a job at QC Homes as a customer service representative solving problems for people who had just bought new homes. I called and asked for an appointment and I got one that afternoon; in the late 1970s that was possible. I spent three hours talking to the manager about my many glowing qualifications for the position, and whatever he threw at me, I handled. Soon he took me in to meet the stogy-puffin' big boss and the two of them talked to me for another hour. I came across as not only efficient, but totally adorable. Lulubelle was being a lady, but she was having fun with them all right!! On this occasion, we seemed to be doing this together and both enjoying it. It turned out that I was qualified—or so they thought. I probably could have done the job quite well, because I am relatively intelligent, but the things I told them I could do were quite embellished from what my true qualifications were. I did not lie to them; I just happened to have Lulubelle's unbridled enthusiasm, which was big enough to make even me think that I could do anything. They offered me the job, and I told them I would let them know in the morning. By then I was back on the ground, Lulubelle had disappeared, and I turned it down. Besides that, I had to go to work in the lab that day. Our nasty follies had filled our day—and wasted theirs!

Another time Lulubelle decided that we should grow some plants. That sounds innocent enough, but nothing was innocent when she was involved. I bought dozens of packs of seeds, multiple bags of dirt, and hundreds of pots. By that time I was married to John, who built me a grow light table, and I began. I planted hundreds of plants, and even succeeded in growing African violets from planting a single leaf. This bout of mania lasted a couple of months. I was obsessed with these plants and just kept planting more and more of them. I had plants sitting everywhere all over my 4000 square foot house and I was actually running out of shelf space. Then the inevitable happened. I woke up one morning only to find that Lulubelle was gone and I, on my own, had plummeted back to earth with no easy landing. I got up, looked at the plants, and hated them. It was all that I could do not to destroy them right there and then; instead, I declared to myself that I would never water them again. I stuck with that decision and they died, one by one. I now have nothing but silk plants in my house and I will never own a living plant again. In fact, every time I have tried to grow a plant of any kind since then, it has justifiably died on me.

Once when Lulubelle got us into doing a large macramé project, I knew that I had to finish it all in one sitting or I would crash and never do it again. I stayed up for 36 hours working on it until it was done. I did not see it as work, of course; I was tying knots as though I were in a frenzy. I finally finished it and literally fell into bed. When I woke up, Lulubelle was gone; the manic obsession was gone and after having worked all those hours, I had no idea how to do macramé anymore. Every time I looked at that huge curtain of knots, I wondered who had done it and how. Believe me; I never touched another macramé knot in my life.

I had many craft binges and the same thing would happen; afterwards, I would look at the project and wonder how I could possibly have done it because I had no memory of the method used whatsoever. That has actually continued in the recent years. One minute totally obsessed, and then nothingness.

That side of Lulubelle, I could handle. It was bothersome, but it did not cause any damage other than some money spent for all the materials, with many of them going to waste. I became so known for my methods of buying all the best supplies for these projects and giving them up that one time my sister-in-law asked me if there was any chance I would be taking up painting soon. I asked her why. She replied that she was interested in painting, but could not afford to buy the supplies. She hoped that I would because when I lost interest I could give the supplies to her. We laughed, but she had a great idea. I had tried everything else and gone crazy buying the appropriate supplies, why not painting? She got the supplies pretty quickly because no amount of manic activity made me a good painter!

Lulubelle also had some good sides. When she was around I could do public speaking, sell anything, entertain people, cook up a storm, be the perfect hostess, and in general be a lot of fun. I will concur, though, that I think I was very tiring to all the people around me because the energy coming off of me was wild.

Then there was the Lulubelle that could attract any man she wanted—she was a misery! Give her a party and she was deadly. That was how she managed to have so many affairs. She did not make life easy for my first husband Dan; the confines of marriage were not to her liking one bit. Lulubelle broke all the rules that I had grown up with and it was great to have someone to blame. There were times that I actually envied her and the fun she had.

I must add here that although it appears otherwise, I really do take full ownership of all the harm and hurt that was done to myself and others at the hands of Lulubelle. I created her to play the roles in life that I could not play, so I am responsible for all of her actions. Lulubelle was the conduit for letting me do the things that would otherwise be taboo. I was Lulubelle. Lulubelle was me. She was like the cousin who did all the things that you had never been allowed to do—you hated her, but you envied her too. Yes, I actually envied a part of myself—that is how different she was than the Judy part of me.

Between marriages, I saw the power of this side of me as far as men were concerned. I could work hard all day and be ready to drop, but as soon as I walked in the door of my apartment at night, Lulubelle would literally jump out of me and she would immediately take over. She would get on the phone and arrange a babysitter, find someone to go out with, and away she would go. She always wore short gorgeous dresses (many of which I sewed for her) with huge earrings. When she walked into any room, she looked around and picked out the man she would go home with. She rarely failed to get him.

One night Lulubelle went out partying wearing an electric blue minidress and her trademark hoop earrings. She really looked wonderful! I always knew that I was quite a plain Jane, but Lulubelle was so much fun that she made us look pretty darned good. One night she brought home a "gentleman" who definitely did not have honorable intentions. They walked into our house and immediately a transformation took place; Judy landed like a rock back into existence.

All of a sudden I was standing in my own apartment with a man whom I did not know. I think that, in the atmosphere of my own home, I was nothing more than a mother and a woman who was struggling to make a life for herself and her two beloved boys. There was no role for Lulubelle to play within these walls. The change of personality was so physically obvious that the man took a step back and said, "Who the Hell are you? Where did she go?" Before I could answer (what could I possibly tell him?), he was out of the door like a shot. Right in front of the door was the staircase going up to the second floor. After the guy left, I looked up and Lulubelle was running up the stairs; when she got to the landing, she turned around with her hands on her hips and said, "You bitch, look what you

Marilyn Avient

did!" She then continued up to the bedroom. In my mind, I can still hear the stomping of her high heels as she flounced up the stairs. As for me, I stood there feeling exhausted. Lulubelle, my alter ego, was one tough gal to live with.

Her stories of conquests were funny, in retrospect, and even admirable to those who had been on the dating scene at the same time that I was. Luckily AIDS had not been heard of yet because she was quite adept at jumping in and out of beds. Or rather, Lulubelle jumped in and I jumped out. Sometimes I felt like I would die of the shame.

On the last night of my loose living—January 1, 1975—I told the guy I was with to throw some money on the dresser and get the Hell out. Because we were at his place, that was difficult, but he did as he was told and left me a $20 bill. Finally, someone had put a dollar figure on my worth. His estimation and mine were not that far apart; his was a few dollars higher than mine. I knew that I had reached a bottom that even Lulubelle could not save us from. I vowed to God my days of sleeping around had come to an end. I guess he heard me … two weeks later.

CHAPTER 8

On January 16th, 1975, I met my second husband, John, and on that day I put Lulubelle into hiding. All of a sudden life took on a whole new light for me. We fell for each rather quickly and moved in together only two weeks after we met. The night we met, John told me about his daughter, Lindsey, who was *the apple of his eye*. However, I did not meet her until 1978 (after John and I were married) when she came back from living overseas with her mother and new stepfather who was in the Canadian Air Force. As you can imagine, all of sudden I was a stepmother to a 16-year-old girl and, while raising two sons, this was a shock to my system. On the other side of the fence, Lindsey instantly had a stepmother who was quite strict and sometimes hard to love. But, over the years, as we both grew up, the strife slowly changed to the point that we came to love each other more and more. Now Lindsey is one of my favorite people; now she is my daughter. And what is even better is that she feels the same about me!

John also had a son, Andrew, who was three years older than Lindsey; he was 18 when I met him. Andrew was difficult, to say the least, from the first day I set eyes on him. I loved him because he was John's son, but he did not make that easy. Suffice it to say that we definitely had a love–hate relationship that put a huge dark cloud over our home while he was in it.

Andrew totally idolized John, but he could not keep his head on straight long enough to become the kind of man that his father could be proud of; he was a drug addict and he was imprisoned three times for drug-related crimes. John loved his son, but could not put up with the heartache anymore so he severed ties with Andrew at the onset of the third prison sentence. Upon being released, Andrew was deported back to Britain (John was born and lived in Wales until he was 27 years old), where he struggled to clean up his life. Only at this time, with the safety of an ocean between us, did Andrew and I begin to get to know each other through letter writing. As much as he tried to better himself (all in hopes of one day seeing his father again to make amends), his self-damaging lifestyle got the better of him. Andrew died in 1994, at the age of 33, when his body simply gave up after too many years of cocaine, heroin, sedatives, and painkillers. (I have a wonderful talk about Andrew's life and how his actions affected us, his family, called "I Choose to Live.")

Looking back, I can hardly believe the thoughtlessness of John and I moving in together so early in our relationship. The boys immediately loved him, and he loved them right back, but they would have been heartbroken if we realized later that we had made a bad mistake and he had to leave. John was a hard-working, fun-loving man who was oh, so easy to love. I knew he was special because almost as soon as I met him, I could feel my childhood rules begin to kick into overdrive. I went directly into fear mode because in my mind I said, "Because I love him I know that he will leave me—like my dad, he may just go off in the night." (For some reason I never reminded myself that my dad came back and that he was away because he was working!) I had to become the *best* at everything so he would not know how to live without me. It was very hard and, most of the time, thankless work because he just thought that I was naturally a person who would move mountains for him or anybody else. He did not realize that I was not moving those darned mountains because I was a good person; rather, I was a desperate one. I would do anything to keep him in the dark about my paralyzing fear because I knew that when he found out, he would be gone!

John worked out of town 80% of the time so I had a lot of respite from the act that I put on when he was around. The only two people in the world who got to see the real me were Sean and Jason; sometimes they felt trapped knowing that they were a part of the conspiracy to keep my secret from John.

One day comes to mind. In about 1982 John went to Las Vegas by himself for a weekend. We did not have much money, so I felt that it was kind of a strange thing to do. I could not understand why he would go off like that by himself. Anyway, in the middle of the night on the first night he was gone, I got a call from the credit department at a Vegas hotel wanting verification that John really was in Las Vegas. Apparently he wanted to take some cash and put it on a credit card. I should have lied, but instead I verified that he was there. The next night I got a second call asking the same thing. In total John probably put $1000 on his credit card that weekend.

I turned into something out of a horror movie. I screamed. I cried. I eventually just lay on the bed unable to move. My first fear was about the money and then I was terrified that he wanted the money so that he could leave me. The boys had to take care of me during this episode. Eventually, after I had been motionless on the bed for many hours, Sean called my friend, Beth, to come over because he was so scared. When she arrived, she got me up and talking. Even she could not believe the range of emotions that I went through in my fearful state that night.

The next day John came home. My boys were home with me when he arrived and later I heard that Sean almost threw up when he saw me greet John. I ran to the door, threw my arms around him, and said, "Hi, Honey, how was your trip?" I bounced about looking great and acting happy, never saying one word about my weekend and how I had reacted to the calls. Only after I was in hospital did Beth tell him about what she saw that day. John had no clue that I could be like that. To Sean and Jason, it was just one of many emotional episodes with me that they had to put up over the years. Looking back, I think they could have handled the episodes if I had shared them with John as well. Sean especially hated the duality of me and how I made them carry the full load while John, the adult, got none of it.

No matter what kind of a wonderful weekend I had with John, I never felt secure when he went back to work. Every Monday, as soon as he left I would, without fail, go into the bedroom and check to see if his favorite clothes were in the closet, if his favorite watch was in its case, and if his Frankie Laine records were still in the rack beside the stereo system. I knew that he would never leave without those things. As long as they were there, he would be back. In other words, in my mind those records, clothes, and jewelry were more important to John than I was. I never felt that I, alone, was enough of a lure to bring him home.

We got married on March 19, 1977, and on April 14 my father passed away. I totally fell to pieces; it was so bad that John told me that if he had known what I would be like in the months after Dad died, he never would have married me. But he *had* married me, and I really did not realize the depth of loyalty in this man because he stayed with me through the whole ordeal of my illness.

John was there for me but he hated every minute of the years in which I was in and out of hospital. In fact, he was downright angry, and he did not know that I knew that. For one thing, he visited me as few times as possible when I was hospitalized. He did not tell any of his work mates that I was unwell, so I knew there was some embarrassment or shame involved. There was also a whole lot of helplessness and a wondering how he was going to spend the rest of his life with a person who was mentally ill. The doctor told him that I was manic-depressive and that I would be in that condition for all of my years. Although I was upset with him a lot in those days because I felt his distress and his anger, I also felt a great deal of sympathy for him because I would not have wanted to be in his shoes. In this respect, I felt that I had the easier load to carry.

John came from a family who did not know the meaning of depression. He was raised with laughter and a carefree outlook on life. How he managed to connect with me is a mystery still. I remember on about the third day I knew him, I asked him if he would babysit the boys for a couple of hours because I had a psychiatrist's appointment. That should have been a clue for him to run far and run fast.

One of the hardest things for John to do was to drive me back to the hospital after a weekend at home. I found out later that he often cried all the way back home—cried for me, for himself, for us, for the boys, because this was not the way he had pictured his life. Reality was very ugly to him and I am still shocked that he stayed. It would not have surprised me if he had taken the boys and left. I would not be the first mental patient to lose her family. There was something very strong and very special about this man whom I had married.

Somehow or other, we have made it through 30 years so far. On our 25th wedding anniversary we held a *huge* gala. As a way of renewing our vows, we both told all our friends how we felt about each other. I would like you to read my speech so that you will see how we fared in the long run.

THROUGH THE YEARS

I would marry John Avient again any time, any place, and under any circumstances. Through the years he has been the love of my life, my best friend, and my favorite person. I am so grateful tonight to have this chance to pay tribute to this man whom I am proud to call my husband.

We would not be celebrating this event tonight if we had merely survived the passage of 25 years while residing in the same house. We are here because we decided that we truly deserve to celebrate tonight because we have grown as individuals and as a couple through the years that we have been together. I am so grateful to have this opportunity to publicly thank John for being in my life. So please, sit back and relax because I have no intention of leaving this spot until I have said all that I need to say about this beautiful man and the life that we have shared.

We are often amazed at how diverse our interests are and how totally different we are in personality. We are living proof that opposites really do attract. However, no matter how dissimilar our interests may be, our values are identical. Although we face opposite directions in many things that we do, somehow we are still walking side by side every step of the way.

I met John Avient at one of the lowest ebbs of my life. I was a divorced mother with two small boys whom I adored with all my heart. I also had a job that I liked a lot and that paid the bills. However, I was searching, searching, and searching for that something else that would fill the void in my life. In that search, I played all the dating games and lost. By January

Marilyn Avient

16, 1975, I had decided that the love I was looking for did not exist and, if it did, it did not have my name on it.

Even when I first set eyes on him, I never even imagined that this handsome, glowing man would ever pay any attention to me. I was wrong and I knew it as soon as we had said no more than a few sentences to one another. I have never believed in love at first sight, but we have not been out of each other's lives since that first moment when we said hello, so call that what you may.

Many years ago, I had a total mental breakdown and I was absent in all the important ways for four years. I was nobody's wife and nobody's mother during that time. One of the things that has cemented our marriage has been the honesty that John gave to me when I was on the road to recovery. He confessed that he probably would not have been able to stick with me the whole way through if he had not been away working so much of the time. Second, he confessed that because I had changed so much he did not feel like I was the girl he married, but he had promised Sean and Jason that he would care for them and so he stayed because of them.

Many marriages would have crumbled with this truth—ours got stronger. I realized that with this confession, I could trust John with absolutely anything that came our way from then on. This man had been brave enough to tell the truth that he had actually lost faith in us, and if he could do that, he would be able to tell me the truth about anything and everything else. That integrity and honesty became our cornerstones from that day forward.

John stands 5 feet 4.5 inches in height, but he has never spent a day of his life feeling or acting short. Most people are surprised when they hear his actual height, because he has a stature that makes him appear 10 feet tall. He has always come across as a no-nonsense kind of guy and as you all know one never wonders where they stand with John Avient. These outer qualities are very evident and well known, but I would like to tell you tonight about the three not-so-well known qualities that I love about this man.

Unpretentious: As you all know, John likes the biggest and the best of everything. He seems to have his own private stock of horseshoes, because he manifests everything he wants in life like no one I have ever seen. However, John never acquires anything as a means of impressing anyone else. He buys what he buys because he, John Avient, wants it. He built me a house at South Cooking Lake—a big house. It was a 4000 square foot bungalow that was 100 feet long. It had a driveway that ran along the whole front of the house because the garage was on the far inside end. When I say that John built this house, I mean it literally. John either pounded or supervised every nail that went into it. On this particular day, he was putting up rafters on the garage when a big, long, black, limousine-like car pulled into the driveway and came all the way in to where he was working. A very well-dressed man got out and commented on the size of the house. John agreed it was big. Then the man asked John when "they" were going to be moving in. Without missing a beat, John said "they" were hoping it would be ready by November of that year. The man then said good-bye and left, not having any idea that John was the owner, and not the hired help. He had assumed that anyone who would build such a large home would not dream of building it himself. John knew it was his house and that was all that was important to him.

Soft Heart: I could tell so many stories on this topic but I shall limit myself to one. For many years while we were at Cooking Lake, there was a hunting rifle on the upper shelf of our closet. I just assumed that John had been a hunter before we met, but as I hate even the idea of killing animals, I did not want to know about it. However, one day after being in the house for many years, I finally got up the nerve to ask about it and this is what he told me. "Years ago, three guys from work asked me to go hunting with them, so I bought this rifle and went. We sat in the bush where we could see a clearing, and waited for an animal to appear. Finally, a beautiful doe stepped into view. I could see the others preparing to shoot, but I couldn't stand it, so I jumped up and yelled, "RUN, YOU SUCKER, RUN!" The doe leapt away to safety. I thought the guys were going to shoot me, but they didn't. They just never asked me to go hunting with them again. I was glad, because I can't kill anything." I cried when I heard the story and I fell in love with him all over again. When we moved out of that house I noticed the rifle was gone.

Spoiling Me: Since the day I met John, I have never wanted for anything; in fact, I learned very early on that I had to be careful in what I said, because if I said I wanted or needed something, he would get it for me whether we could afford it or not. I have one particular incident that will always make me smile whenever I think about it.

About 20 years ago I gave John my wish list at Christmastime. One of the things I asked for was a set of mixing bowls. I loved to bake and needed more bowls than the ones I owned. I knew that he could get a nice set at Zellers for no more than $20 at that time. On Christmas morning it came as no surprise that I got everything on my list and more, including a set of bowls. When I opened the very large box that contained the bowls, I saw that they were unlike any that I had seen before. The largest was gigantic and the other two were smaller but still good sized. On the bottoms I saw that they were made in England and I also noticed that John had left the price tags on. The smallest one cost $75, the next was $100, and the largest was $125. My set of three bowls cost a total of $300. I gasped and told John that I loved them, but a $20 set from Zellers would have been just fine. He put his arms around me and said, "Nothing but the best for my girl; nothing but the best!

There are two huge things that I need to thank John for at this time. First of all, this man has supported me financially and emotionally in every project I have undertaken, and I never do anything without expending a lot of money to make sure that I have the very best tools for whatever it is that I want to do. He may weary of this on the inside, but he rarely lets me know about it. When I do something I go into it full tilt and John just patiently waits for me to slow down and drop back to earth. He makes me feel safe.

The other thing that John has done is not only give me the best of himself, but by doing so he has shown me the best of myself. Every day he shows me that I am worth more than the going rate, just as he did with the bowls. Every day, I feel his sentiments of "Nothing but the best for my girl! Nothing but the best." I respect him and his opinion so much that when he says that I am lovable and important, I wonder, "What if he is right?" When he tells me how talented and gifted I am, I have wondered, "What if he is right?" When he tells me that there is nothing on earth that I could not do if set my mind to it, I have wondered, "What if he is right?" Finally, one day recently I realized that by loving me so completely, he actually taught me how to love myself. So I get the best of him, and I end up with the best of myself as well. It just doesn't get any better than that.

In conclusion, I would like to share with you a poem that I wrote about John in 1991.

MY HUSBAND

A simple man, yet complex.
A humble man, yet proud.
A stubborn man, yet yielding.
A giving man, yet always holding back.
Sometimes, not often,
I get to see the little boy who romped the hills of Wales.
I see the tender, vulnerable heart
That his mother knew and loved.
But, mostly, I see the man,
The hard worker, the provider.

Marilyn Avient

I see weariness.

I see frustration.

I see dreams unrealized.

I also see strength unlike any other.

I see loyalty unfamiliar to most.

I see depth that would challenge any ocean.

I see love wrapped like a secret present.

This man, my husband, is my connection to the earth.

No matter how high I fly,

I am safe-

He is waiting on the ground, feet firmly planted.

My man wants to give me so much-

He wants to give me the world.

My man is a silly man-

All I ever really wanted was HIM.

THROUGH …

The walls were lined with cobwebs
And reeked the stench of neglect.
No wisp of air; no sign of love;
No life could I detect.
For years I sat in darkness,
I floundered and gasped for air.
I waited for someone to find me;
I waited for someone to care.

Excerpt from
"Happiness Where Are You?"
The Girl Behind the Closed Door
by Marilyn Avient

CHAPTER 9

As mentioned in the previous chapter, my father died in 1977, and although I grieved deeply for him, I never really dealt with his death. The seven-year anniversary of that event occurred within 14 days of the date of my first hospitalization, and that is not surprising as seven years is how long it takes for unresolved issues to come to fruition. So in early 1984, my dad's death was something that should have been resolved, but was not. Around the first of March that year, I knew I was at a lower ebb than I had ever been before and I was terrified. I went to Calgary for a week with John thinking that maybe I needed a change of scenery and some time to rest during the day when he was at the job site. It was pleasant enough in that I saw more of John than usual, but I was sad—very, very sad. John knew that something was wrong, but I made sure that he did not know to what extent I was falling apart inside.

One particular day stands out in my mind shortly after I got home. I had recently been to see my family doctor a few times and we had talked, so she knew that I was in a low mental state. On this particular day, for some reason, I decided that *all* of the glassware in my house needed cleaning. Instead of bringing out a few things at a time, I brought every piece (and there were hundreds) into the kitchen and lined my cupboards and island with them. I had 30 feet of cupboards and every inch was covered with glassware. Then I looked at them and decided that all I wanted to do was smash every one of them. I started to cry hysterically as I desperately tried to keep myself under control so that I did not do any damage. Somehow in the midst of all that, I managed to get myself to the phone to call my doctor. She offered to send her nurse out to my home to take me to the psychiatric clinic in Edmonton, but between sobs I told her that I could get myself there. I never did like people doing things for me.

Just then I heard the front door open, and John called out, "Hi, Honey! Is the coffee pot on?" He was on his way from the Edmonton office to a job site in eastern Alberta and he dropped in because he was passing right by our place on the way out of town. In the time it took for him to walk from the front door to the kitchen (about 30 steps) I stopped crying, put on a smile, and poured us some coffee. In those days I smoked, so we sat down and had a coffee and a cigarette together. He asked if I was OK and I assured him I was great. He commented on the big job I had undertaken with the glassware, then said he had to hit the road. I kissed him good-bye, and as soon as he was gone, I got on my coat and headed for the clinic in Edmonton. I cried all the way there. I was such an expert at changing my facade for John that I had not missed a beat in transforming my mood for him. You will recall how this behavior infuriated my sons because they would see me falling to pieces while John always got to see me smiling.

At the clinic they talked to me, then did an electroencephalography (EEG) to make sure that my brain was working properly. I would have to wait about 10 days for the results. Before I ever heard from them with any conclusions about the state of my brain, I would see my doctor a couple more times. Finally, on March 28, she said that she was going to talk to a psychiatrist friend of hers to see if he would put me in hospital for a couple of days. I was shocked, but agreed, feeling more than a little relief. When I told John that I needed to go hospital for a few days, he was stunned. He asked me how this could develop this far without him knowing, and I just shook my head. How could I tell him that I had basically been lying to him for years?

The next morning was Sean's 15th birthday and we were having a big dinner for him. Because she knew that I was not feeling well, Mom had kindly offered to take care of the food, and for that I was so very grateful. The only other guests were going to be my stepdaughter, Lindsey, and her husband, Oneil, but it still felt too overwhelming for me to handle by myself.

That morning as I was making lunches for myself and the boys, John asked me if his jeans had been laundered because he would need them the next morning to go out of town. I could hear the edge to his voice and I was scared that he was mad at me for what I had told him the night before about not being well. I said that I would find his jeans and scurried to the bedroom like a little mouse. He came looking for me when I did not return to the kitchen and found me sitting on the floor in the midst of all the dirty laundry. The jeans were in my arms and clasped to my chest. I was rocking backing and forth. When he asked what I was doing, I looked at him and said, "I found your jeans but I just can't remember how to get them to the washing machine." I never felt so helpless in all my life. In fact, that was the moment when I knew there was no life left in me and that I was really, really sick. Still, I could not let John know. He said it was OK about his jeans. Looking back, I have no recollection when or if those jeans ever got washed. The funny thing was that neither of us suggested that I should stay home and get some rest. We both just went off to work as though nothing had happened.

I remember driving down the highway on my way to work praying that God would help me get through the day. I was all right for a short time at work, but all of a sudden everything changed. I went to see Beth at her desk and told her that John was going to leave me. Of course that was not true, but I felt like it was and I completely fell to pieces. I went hysterical. She ran over to my doctor's office to see what she should do. They told her to bring me over. In the meantime, the doctor phoned the psychiatrist; he said that I should be admitted to hospital that day. Beth phoned John and at my request he agreed to meet me at our house. From there he drove me to hospital in total wonderment how his wife could be falling to pieces while he knew nothing about it. I would not let him stay with me at the hospital as I was waiting to be admitted. I wanted to be on my own and told him I would call him when I was settled in. He hates hospitals, so that suited him fine. I had come back to my "take-charge self" so I was able to handle this.

Previously I had phoned Sean and told him that I would have to miss his birthday dinner. He was very upset. He begged me to wait until the next day, but I knew that if I had to be phony for one more night, the results could be devastating. I asked him to understand, but I forgot that, in reality, he was still a child. All he could see was a steamroller slowly moving towards us and he was powerless to stop it. I lost all compassion for anybody that day and wanted to get away from them all. That is partly why I was glad to be at the hospital alone; I did not want to have to take care of John's feelings. For once, I wanted to feel what *I* was feeling.

I was scared about one thing. I had never seen this doctor and I was sure that when he saw me, he would say that there was nothing wrong and would thus send me home to face life on my own again. I was not sure what I would do if that happened. To my dismay, I was told that I would not be seeing him until the next morning when he did his rounds. For the next 18 hours I was very anxious, to say the very least.

In the meantime, I had to get settled in for at least one night's stay in this place. The psych ward was nothing like in the movies. It was modern, spacious, clean, bright, and very pleasant. I was given a room all to myself and that was a relief. I noticed groups of patients sitting together, but no one was very friendly. On psych wards, patients wear their street clothes, and so do the nurses. I found out later that I looked so "together" that the patients thought I was a new nurse on the ward; that was why they were so unfriendly to me. That night I got asked dozens of questions by the intake nurse; I kept waiting for her to assure me that I would be staying for a while. She was pleasant, but very professional and did not tell me anything, one way or the other.

I sat on a couch by the window and got yelled at by a patient; this scared the Hell out of me. Then I sat in another place and watched a few of the older patients walk in a big circle for what seemed like hours. They all looked drugged to me, but after a few days, they looked perfectly normal.

That night I was too nervous to sleep and I was very surprised, and very relieved, to see my mom come through the door to visit me. She said she had to see for herself that I was all right. She said that the dinner had gone fine, albeit quieter than usual. I asked how everyone reacted to me being here, and she said it was not even talked about. I could hardly believe it. *Our family's chief cook and bottle washer was in the loony bin and no one talked about it!* I was hurt. I was shocked. I was mad—in more ways than one! Later I was told that the scene was one of subdued shock. No one knew what to say and they did not want to spoil Sean's birthday—as though that had not already been done!

Apparently Beth went over later in the evening and talked to Sean. She also arranged to meet with John to fill him in on all that she knew about what I was going through. I assumed that if they met for coffee or lunch, they would have an affair. I wanted her to talk to him, but I feared I was going to lose him. When she arrived to see me the morning after I was admitted, I talked as though it was fait accompli that she would be heading off into the sunset with John. I remember going into acceptance of that because I could not do anything about it—I was too sick to put out any effort one way or the other. I had kept John away from my friends because I assumed that as soon as he was alone with one of them, I would lose him. I am sad when I realize the vast extent of the fear that was in my every waking hour during those years. What a way to live! Actually, I was not living at all; I was merely surviving at the most basic level.

That morning I met the psychiatrist, Dr. A. We talked for about an hour. At the end of it, he told me that the hospital was exactly where I should be and that I would probably be there for about six weeks, if not longer. He also said that I would not be put on any medication until I had been assessed fully. That gave me confidence in him. Only at that moment did I give myself permission to break down. I had been keeping myself together so that in the event he sent me home, I would still be able to function. Now I was safe. Now I was away from all the pressures of life. Now I was off the stage. Now I could crash and someone would catch me. Now I was free to go inside and stay there until I wanted to come out. I am glad that I had no idea how very long the road was going to be to get back to anything resembling "normal." First, however, I would have to venture even further away before I could start the long trek home.

The first days in the hospital were filled with tests, tests, and more tests. They tested me for medical purposes and I tested them to see where their boundaries were and to see how safe this place really was. I remember sitting looking at a long blank wall that extended for about 40 feet across the main room where we all gathered for meals. Upon reflection now, it had to have some doors in it because bedrooms surrounded the main gathering area, but in my memory of looking at it then I do not see any doors. I see a blank wall just begging to be not so blank. Every meal I looked at it and thought about how I would love to throw something at it. I asked a favorite nurse one morning what the punishment would be if someone were to, accidentally on purpose, flick an egg off of one's plate onto that wall so that it slithered down the boring white surface. She replied, "Most people would get into trouble for it, but we would probably cheer if you did it." I never did it after that because I knew it would be OK to do it. I should not have asked. I should have just done it, but I did not take risks in those days—none at all.

I loved having a room all to myself, knowing that I could go in and out whenever I wanted to; I could stay up all night; I could talk to myself; I could sit on the floor and pout or play or cry or laugh or sing and no one would see me or hear me. In that first stay, I found myself hoarding things in my storage locker. In those days I smoked heavily and every time Beth came up to see me, I would ask her to bring me a carton of cigarettes. I would also tell John to do the same. Very soon I had about ten cartons of cigarettes hidden away and every day I would take them out and count them and then cover them up and put them back. I had other treasures hidden there too. Lindsey brought me a beautiful ornament and I should have put it out to enjoy it, but instead, I wrapped it up and put it in the cupboard right along with my cigarettes. Every day I would take it out and look at it, love it, and then wrap it up and put it back safely on its shelf. These things were for my eyes only and I absolutely loved having things that were mine, mine, mine. No one else had any say over what was in that cupboard; that was my domain. This act of hiding things away for only my eyes to see has lasted in differing degrees to this day. Some things still never make it to a shelf. These hidden treasures used to be the gauge of my self-worth and represented my degree of freedom in the world. That is not saying much about myself, if that is how I measured me. However, it told me that I had never felt like I had owned anything in my life because that is something that I pounced on as being important. Today, it just feels like a delicious secret between me and . . . me.

My first hospitalization was also characterized by the fact that no one could sit close to me. I would go into panic attacks if anyone even sat in a chair right beside me. I would have to tell the person to please move over to the next chair; if he or she would not move—then I did. Some people were offended by my need to have no one touch me, but others just saw me as crazy and they complied, so it was no problem. I had this fear that if anyone sat that close they might touch me and I was convinced that even a touch would take a piece of me away. I had given so much of myself away over the years that I felt like there was not much left to give.

My fears were realized one night when I was in my room sitting on my bed; I looked down and my arms were gone. In my eyes, and to my mind, I was literally disappearing, one limb at a time. I rang the bell for the nurse and when she answered over the speaker, I just screamed, "Come quickly, I'm disappearing. Oh, God, I'm disappearing." She came in, but to my astonishment she did not get excited and she tried to settle me down with platitudes. I saw immediately that I would have to handle this problem on my own, but I had no idea how I was going to do that. Nonetheless, I came up with a strategy. I was now thoroughly convinced that if anybody touched me, that part of me would start to vanish bit by bit, just as my arms had done. As I said before, people had been taking bits of me for a long time but this was the first time that I realized it was now happening on a physical level.

THE HAVEN

One day I slipped away from them.
They knew not where I went.
I went inside to a place all mine,
My feelings all long spent.
I found a haven of darkness
So safe and so secure.
I felt so small and fragile,
Not one touch could I endure.
My being started to disappear,
I dared not close my eyes.
Slowly, slowly . . . nearly gone.
Is this how a body dies?
With terror as my only friend,
I said, "Death would be best."
God smiled at me and shook His head,
"Not now, Child, get some rest."

So I decided that from then on, there would definitely be no touches, no hugs from anyone, and the distance between me and someone sitting at the table became two chair widths. I never told anyone else again about my arms disappearing, and to their minds, the problem had been solved. I can just imagine what the nurses had to say about it: "That Judy is nuttier than we gave her credit for!" There are times, even now, when I still just want to be in my own little space, but nothing like I did then. I think it is something all of us want once in a while to some degree. Today, however, I tend to get a little panicky if I have done a lot of giving to the point of feeling depleted on all levels. I usually am successful in getting past this by taking some time to myself and holding back a little more when I am around people. I also get tired of the constant hugging that the women of today do when they merely say hello or good-bye. Some days, I just subtly back away, so that the person knows I do not want a hug and is not insulted.

One evening Beth and I were sitting in my room enjoying a visit when the head nurse knocked on the door. She came to ask me if I would be willing to give up my single room and move to one that I would be sharing with another woman. I thought I was going to pass out right there in front of her and Beth. My heart began to race, my body instantly became clammy and sweaty; I thought and wished that I would just disappear to anywhere but there. I finally asked why and who and when, then curled up on the bed and sobbed. I begged Beth to take me home with her and to please not make me stay in this awful place.

The scene does not appear to be too dramatic on the written page, but in reality the wailing and the begging went on for over an hour. Finally, I was exhausted from the raw emotion of it all. After a while the nurse said that I should not worry about it anymore because they would find another solution. Beth and I then went out to the main room for a coffee. While we were sitting there a woman named Joyce came over to talk to us. I was surprised because she seemed to be held hostage in her own little world and had not talked to me before. She said to Beth, "Don't worry about your friend here; I'll take care of her. They try to bully you around here, but I don't ever let them make me do anything I don't want to do. I'll keep an eye on her because I can see she needs some protecting." Joyce and I became fast friends for the time that we were in hospital, but I never knew what happened to her after that.

Later that evening after the lights went down, the head nurse came in to see if I was OK after all the ruckus. I was totally exhausted, but I had settled down. She said something to me that I have never forgotten: "You know, Judy, *all you had to do was say NO*." I asked her if it had been some kind of a test. She said, "No, but if we had known that you were going to react so extremely, it would have been." They never again asked me to change rooms or do anything else of the sort. Until that incident I had no idea just how much my privacy meant to me. Where had all these emotions been hiding? I had never reacted to anything in my life the way I reacted that night. What was still to come?

During my first stay in hospital, Beth was my friend, my ally, my protector, my connection with the outside world. I relied on her for a lot and she always came through. Some of my memories about this period come from her because my memory dims on certain events. For instance, she tells me that we used to go to the cafeteria for a coffee and I would literally huddle in the corner of the booth. I would hunch my shoulders and hug myself, like I was hanging on for dear life. I remember the feeling but I cannot truthfully say that I remember displaying it that way.

Every day the doctor would come in and talk. I remember one session when I must have been telling about my unique ways of handling relationships and he told his resident, "Go out and find me a big cross because we have a martyr here to crucify!" Of course, he was referring to me and I was shocked to be called such a thing. I was even more astounded later when I realized that he was right.

After about two weeks, I was allowed to go out on a day pass, so John and the boys came to get me. We went to West Edmonton Mall where John bought me a really nice casual jogging suit that he figured would be perfect for wearing at the hospital. We each had a soft drink and while sitting in the food court, I became extremely claustrophobic. It was all I could do to beg John to get me out of there and fast. He did as I asked and we went to Lindsey's for the rest of the day. I was not really interested in visiting and it seemed that John and the boys felt the same way. However, if they had to be in this situation, they wanted to be anywhere other than alone with me, because they did not know what to do with me in my present state of mind. They felt better trying to visit me in the midst of familiar people. I have since been told that I did not want to sit with them either because I sat behind the couch on the floor and smoked; all that could be seen of me was the smoke rising up from my chain-smoked cigarettes. That really is quite funny not only because it was a weird thing to do but also because Lindsey did not allow smoking in her house. This must be true, because both she and John verify it, but I do not remember the incident at all.

By afternoon, long before my curfew, I asked John to take me back to the hospital; he was happy to comply. When we got there we could not find a parking stall, so I told them to just let me out at the front door. John told Sean to take me up to the ward and he would keep driving around until he came back down. I did not kiss or hug anyone good-bye because I could not be touched, not even by them. Up on the ward in front of the nurses' station, I told Sean that he could leave me there because I did not want to go to my room yet. I said good-bye and turned to walk away (very unlike the old me) but, instead of following my implied wishes, he grabbed me and hugged me and kissed me good-bye. He was only 15 years old and the nurses at the desk were visibly shocked. I still did not want anyone to touch me, but he did break a small hole in the ice. After Sean left one of the nurses said, "Have you any idea what a special boy your son is? Not many kids his age could have done what he just did."

I was not surprised by Sean's maturity and his innate ability to do what most kids would never dream of doing because he had been doing these things for a very long time. One incident stands out for me. Sean was 4 years old and Jason was 2 when their father Dan and I split up while living in British Columbia. I had to put in my last shift at the hospital lab on the day the boys and I were to leave on the long drive to Edmonton, so we did not get away until late in the afternoon. The young man who was boarding in the basement of our house needed a ride to Calgary, Alberta, so I was pleased that I would have adult company for at least that far. I had decided that because we would get there around midnight, I would find a motel for me and my sons to stay in.

The boys slept most of the way to Calgary and that was a blessing for them because they were understandably very sad at leaving their father behind. When we got to Calgary, we dropped our "hitchhiker" off at his parents' home and I proceeded to look for accommodations. No luck! The Calgary

Stampede was on and there was not a room available anywhere in the whole city. I sat in the parking lot of the last motel I tried and I cried—out of sadness, out of weariness, out of frustration, and out of fear.

Sean heard me crying and climbed into the front seat. He asked me what was wrong and he had that wise look on his face that said, "I really want to know, Mom." So, in between my "ugly cry" sobs I told my troubles to my 4-year-old. He looked deep in thought for a few minutes and then he said, "Here is what we'll do. We will go to Edmonton now and I will sit here and I will watch you very closely. If you start to look sleepy, I will poke your arm and you will have to stop the car. If you show me how to read the clock I will wake you after 10 minutes go by. Then you can drive again until the next time I stop you." That dear child stayed awake for the whole four hours that it took to drive to Edmonton and he did exactly as he said he would do. He made me stop three times and each time he woke me exactly 10 minutes later. When we pulled into Edmonton, we both cheered and I said a little prayer of gratitude. As the Bible says, "And a little child shall lead them . . . ."

And now back to the hospital. The doctor was not really sure what to do with me as far as medications went. He determined that I was clinically depressed, but he had trouble deciding if I was a classic depressed person or a bipolar manic depressant, which was more tedious to treat. For some reason, I wanted to be manic depressant rather than just depressed. I think the more elaborate label gave more credibility to the pain that I had always suffered. To be labeled as a manic depressant would justify spending all that money and all that time on projects that I started in frenzy and ended in severe melancholy. I think I even thought it sounded romantic to be considered something that could be potentially dangerous. The nurses even told me that they enjoyed having manic patients. They said that when manic depressive patients were down they were not very interesting, but when they were up, they were a real hoot. I wanted someone to see me as a real hoot. So far that was certainly not happening!

After about ten days, Dr. A. finally decided that I had bipolar affective disorder, or manic depression as it was commonly called then. I am embarrassed to say that I was thrilled with the diagnosis. I had always felt unwell and now I had a label to make it official. On that day, I received my license to be sick for the rest of my life. On that day, I began taking Lithium and a strong antidepressant. Strangely, it was one of the happiest days of my life up to that point. John, however, was not so happy. He went to see Dr. A. and was told that this condition was a *lifelong sentence* so he should get used to it. John said to me later that he did not know what he was going to do because the girl he had married was gone and this child/stranger had taken her place.

Lithium was not a fun drug to take at first. While they were trying to adjust the levels, I was forced to go through the stage of experiencing too high of a dose one day to too low of a dose the next. When it was too high, I shook all over. My teeth even felt like they were rattling. My voice shook when I spoke and the metallic taste in my mouth was just plain awful. Finally, when the correct dosage was established, it became a nonevent to take the Lithium every day. In fact, it became quite humdrum and the "romantic" nature of this condition began to wear thin.

The psychiatric ward was not an unpleasant place to be. We even had little social gatherings such as dances. One evening, John was up to visit me. It was a Thursday and everyone knew that Thursday night was Dance Night. The patients loved it because it was a social situation in which everyone could participate, even those who were in wheelchairs. John and I got up to dance and I was having a good time. In fact, I was just happy to be doing something with my husband. All of a sudden John stopped and said in my ear, "I can't bloody believe it. I'm dancing with a bunch of nuts." I started to laugh hysterically, because I knew how much he hated that place, but I was hurt and I think I chose to laugh because to cry with that same velocity would have flooded the room. John hated what was happening to me; he, who could usually repair anything, was unable to fix me. He did not stay long after that.

I much preferred being where I was rather than living life from John's vantage point. He always reminds me of the time he and the boys came to visit me and I never spoke one word to them. That visit was the one that told him his wife was truly crazy, I think. I remember that visit and I did know that they were there. I was hiding deep inside of myself just at the time and I did not feel like resurfacing for anyone—not even them. I observed them and felt like I could even observe myself from a place outside the scene. They talked among themselves for a while, and then they became too sad to continue. I had always been such a talker that it made them upset to know I had neither the wish nor the ability to respond to them. I was content where I was, and I just could not be there for them that day.

After I had been in hospital for a couple of weeks, I was told that I had to attend group therapy. That sounded scary, but it was an order rather than an invitation, so off I went. However, I was not prepared for what awaited me there. For the first time in my life I was met with blatant hostility from another human being. One of my fellow patients, who I thought was one of my "friends," stood up and demanded that I be kicked out of the group session and out of the hospital as well. She declared in no uncertain terms that I was not one of them and did not deserve to take up the time of the therapists, nurses, or doctors when I had no need for them. When the therapist asked her what she meant, the patient said, "Judy is not one of us. There is no reason for her to be here. She has a husband, a nice house, a profession, good kids, a new car, and no one ever slammed her around when she was a kid. She even has two f—g dogs."

I could not believe my ears and, of course, I began to cry. I thought for sure they were going to do as she had demanded. The therapist explained that if I had all those things and still needed to be there, then I was probably sicker than any of them. That statement set me back on my heels and silenced those who had complained. I never heard another word along those lines again.

What I discovered in group therapy was that I could have been a therapist myself, because I was really good at focusing in on other people's problems. Sometimes I found things that no one else, not even the therapist, was bringing to the surface. On the last session that one man was in, he publicly thanked me and said that if it had not been for me he would never have figured out some of his problems. He then said, "You should be a therapist." The therapist on duty concurred with his evaluation. I was proud of myself for a moment, and then I trivialized it. However, I wished that I could do for myself what I did for numerous other patients in that group.

Every week the patients went out as a group to a social function of some sort. This was done on a volunteer basis and I chose to have no part of it. I did not want to be seen in public as part of a group from a psych ward, even though no one would know who we were and where we had come from. The idea of going with them made me nauseous and I adamantly refused to go. I think it reminded me of the group in the movie *One Flew Over the Cuckoo's Nest* when they went out on their disastrous outing. I did not mind being mentally ill on my own, but I did not want to be seen as one of a bunch.

As in any other part of life, there were rules to follow and punishments for those who did not obey. Being a rules follower, I knew that I did not need to worry about repercussions for my actions in this environment. However, I did develop a big—no, HUGE—fear of some of the consequences. If we were late arriving back from passes without a good excuse, or if we took pills that were not prescribed for us, the punishment was that we would be sent to "lock-up" on the third floor of the hospital. Those who had been there loved to really make it sound awful, so that those of us who had never been there would see them as braver than ourselves just because they had survived such a fate. I used to drive myself into panic attacks over that dreaded place. One girl I knew got sent there because she had taken a number of over-the-counter painkillers all at once. We never saw her again, so who knew what happened to her there!

The other threat even worse than the first was that, if we really got out of line or were totally disobedient, we would be sent to Alberta Hospital. That threat sent chills up my spine. I had grown up in Edmonton and when I was a kid, that horrible place was called Oliver, a place from which, they say, no one ever returned. We were led to believe people were put in cells, not rooms, and everyone was drugged out of their minds. I imagined screaming patients and foul-smelling rooms with all kinds of filth strewn all over the place. This picture probably came to me from the movies or from a past life experience, but I was taking no chances. I behaved myself. The only time I knew of a patient being sent there was during my third hospital stay and this woman was too far gone to be among us. I was afraid of her, and did not want her anywhere around me, but I got sick to my stomach when I literally saw the "men in the white coats" take her away.

One thing that really stood out for me during those six weeks was that I was very exhausted from the myriad of details that I had to contend with in my everyday life. (And, yes, I know that I am not alone in having all these details to think about.) For example, I remember sitting in my favorite spot in front of the huge windows overlooking the road that passes in front of the hospital. During rush hour on that particular day, I was sitting in my cocoon watching the world go by. When I saw woman and a boy in a car, I thought, "She's probably taking him to get his hair cut. I don't have to do that anymore." Perhaps the next car would have a person alone and I would come up with some other errand that he or she probably was doing, one that I used to have to do. I did that with almost every car that passed by, giving one of my duties to each of them. I was so relieved to not be worrying about the little details of life anymore.

IN SEARCH OF SERENITY

I want to find Serenity-
Can you show me the way?
North or South or East or West?
Should I arrive by night or by day?
I have walked down many paths in life,
But none have taken me to this place
Where my heart can play in the morning sun

And at night, sleep in its own special space.
In Serenity, there are no watches or clocks,
No appointments or things to be done.
No one will tell me what I should be doing-
No work, no demands-only fun!
In this place where I long to be,
I'll call the squirrels and ducks by name.
The birds will chirp their awareness of me,
Wild creatures, to me, will be tame.
In Serenity, there are no clouds of grey,
Just white billows in a sky so blue,
And in this place, no rain will fall.
God gives moisture in the form of dew.
Is there a place like this on Earth
Or is it a dream of the very best kind?
I think if I want this freedom of heart,
I must create such a place in my mind.

Another aspect of life that I was happy to be without was cooking. I must have cooked one meal or entertained one person too many because on an inner level I wished for that responsibility to go right out of my life. I was so effective in my wish to relieve myself of those culinary duties that I completely forgot *how* to cook and I had no recollection of what foods my family liked to eat. I took years to get my cooking skills back and when I did, they were completely different. The entertaining never did resume to the point it had been prior to March 1984, but I think it came back to a level that was more comfortable. Today I rarely have company over because even now my nerves get shot in the worry of it.

During my first stay in hospital, I was known to be quiet and shy—except in group therapy—so that was all the other patients expected of me. One day I was lying on my bed, when I looked up, and "saw" Lulubelle standing there in her typical stance of hands on her hips with a glint of mischief in her eye. She said, "Well, are you going to lie there like a lump or do you want to have some fun?" I knew what she meant and I knew what I had to do. I changed my clothes into the new outfit John had bought me, put on some makeup, and curled my hair. Lulubelle just sat there patiently until finally I was ready. I looked the best I had in many weeks.

We left the room. As we got to the large patient area, I surprised everyone by calling out, "Come on everybody. Please take a seat around the big table." They had no idea what was coming because I had always talked very softly, at times inaudibly. Out of curiosity, they did as I asked.

When they were all seated—there were about 20 in total—I stood up at the end of the table and let Lulubelle take over. She amazed them with stories and jokes; they were all laughing and having an unbelievable time. As time went on, various people started saying things like "Where have you been hiding this side of you?" "Why haven't you let us see this person before?" "You are another person entirely!" "We really like you this way." The more they said, the more uncomfortable I became. My stomach started to hurt. My head began to feel like it was in a vice. I got up and ran back to my room, knowing Lulubelle was running after me.

When I got to my room, I started to rant and rave, "You bitch! You did it again! They love you! Everyone bloody loves you! Why, why, why can't anyone love *me* more for once? I hate you! I hate you! I hate you! Now *get out* and never come back."

While I was yelling and crying, I was washing my face and scratching it with my fingernails. When that did not feel harsh enough, I took the nail brush and started trying to remove all traces of the person that others saw and liked instead of me. I scrubbed until I was exhausted; when the pain of my skin outdid the pain in my heart, I stopped. I spent the rest of the day in my room feeling shame, too tired to move. I also did not want anyone asking about the performance that they assumed came from me. I hoped that by tomorrow it would all be forgotten in the maze of pills and self-centered emotions. I do not remember any staff members talking to me about what happened or about my red, raw, and scratched face.

For the most part, the staff members on the psychiatric ward were very nice and I never saw any overt acts of unkindness done to any of the patients. However, the vast majority of the nurses and doctors were not there because they had a calling; the reason they were there was no deeper than the taking home of a paycheck. One day this became painfully obvious to me.

The nurses talked with us individually for a set amount of time each day because that was the rule. At first I thought they were honestly interested in our collective welfare, and that they really liked getting down to the root of our problems. After each of our half-hour talks, the nurse was required to write down all that was said; it was kept as part of our permanent hospital file. They always took notes as we chatted, then transcribed them later into our official files.

That night my nurse for the day, whom I really liked because she seemed to be one who really cared about the patients, came in and asked me to read something on a page out of the file book. I read it and then looked at her questioningly. She said, "I thought this was probably what you would say tonight, and so I wrote it out early. I have a date tonight and don't want to stay late writing up patient's files. So if you think this is what you might have said, then I will file it that way." I was shocked. For one thing, I cringed to think what she and the other nurses must think of me (and the other patients) if I am that predictable. To her my illness was a chore and something so unimportant that she could write up my words before I even said them. If I had been in my "right mind" I would have reported her, but I accepted her put-down as part of life.

You will recall the male nurse who told me that the mental health system was not designed to cure people; its only aim was to "fix" them well enough so that they could leave and make room for those waiting in line. He described it as the "revolving door system of mental health" because you come in, go out, and then, in all probability, come back in again. You just keep going around and around with the door. I was warned, but I still became a part of that system and that door would keep revolving for me for another three years.

CHAPTER 10

I cooperated with the system and made room for another patient on May 15, 1984. Going home was not the happy experience that one would think. Rather, leaving the place that had become my refuge was one of the hardest things I ever had to do. I knew what to expect in hospital; I got told what to do. Conversely, I was going to a place, my home, where I had to tell others what needed to be done. I hated that. I had always been in charge, and all I really wanted was for someone to tell *me* what to do and to take the burden off of my shoulders.

What I did when I got home was to refuse to do some of the things that I had always done. I declared that I was never going to pick another weed in my life and if anyone did not like that, they could do it themselves. My flowerbeds were 100 feet long and about 8 feet wide, so I am talking major weed picking. My mother ended up doing it for a while until I decided that it was a relaxing thing to do in the dark of night. I am not kidding! It could be pitch black and I would be out there pulling weeds with just the crickets to talk to.

I continued to see Dr. A. on a regular basis, but other than prescribing pills and keeping me in the "sick" mode, he was quite useless. He was the one who had three rules for the therapy sessions in his office: No talking about my childhood; no talking about religious beliefs; no talking about the future. I was only allowed to tell him about what I had done since my last visit with him. I have been in enough therapy to know that this was a very strange way to work with a patient. Sigh!

One time when I went to see Dr. A. at his office, he refused to let me get to the root of the fear that I was feeling that day and I was afraid to leave the office when we were done. I told the receptionist that I was scared to leave and she relayed that to the doctor. He told me I could sit in the back room for a while. Well, his back room ended up being the room where they stored their office supplies and where the copier was located. There was no chair, so I huddled in the corner, on the floor, for an hour or so. Soon the receptionist told me I had to leave because they were closing up for the day. That dear old doctor did not even come in to see if I, his patient, was all right. They sent me home and I felt like they were sending me to the black pit without a shovel.

My family seemed happy to have me home from the hospital, but I am sure they had as much trepidation about it as I did, only for different reasons. In many ways I was a stranger to them and they were not at all sure they wanted the new me in their home on a full-time basis. Just as they had many questions about what I was willing or able to do, I had many questions of my own. What would they expect of me? Would I have to go back to the same old routine? Did they expect me to cook? Did they expect me to act like an adult? Did they expect me to drive the boys around? Did they expect me to go back to work in the lab? The questions were endless and the answers were slow in coming.

The one thing that made the transition a little easier was that it was mandatory for me to attend a seven-week day therapy program that was held at the same hospital where I had lived for six weeks. The hours were from 9 am to 4 pm Monday through Friday, so that we had to develop a routine that was reminiscent of going off to work every day. I am sure this was not by accident because the purpose of this course was to prepare us for life back in the outside world. I loved this course. I felt quite grown up going out each morning and returning late in the day, quite happy to have a home to return to after a hard day of being in touch with my emotions. I tried to put on the air that I was going to and from work, as though anyone at the bus stop really cared. Only on a couple of occasions did I wish that I could go to my room on the ward, because on those days I really needed a safe cocoon to curl up in and "home" did not always fit the bill.

Following those seven weeks, John took me, Sean, and Jason on a car trip to Ontario where we visited my sister, Barbara, and her family. We had a good time, but I found it very hard to be so out of my safety zone, which had become very enclosed during the past months. I went wherever I was told to go during our time in Ontario, and for the most part enjoyed just being with my family.

When we got back to Alberta, John and I went to Kokanee Springs with another couple for a few days of golf. I did not know this other couple, so it really was a trial by fire for me. I did not golf and was thankfully left all alone for hours at a time. I rejoiced in my solitude because I did not have to pretend to be normal (whatever that is). I had a tablecloth I was working on, so I immersed myself in the act of creation, which is always a saving grace for me. I knew they did not know I had been sick so recently and I did not tell them because I knew John wanted it that way. I believe there was still some shame on John's part because he did not know how to be proud of someone whom he saw as childlike and weak.

After one of my hospital stays, John made a reference about me being weak. No matter how I was feeling before he said it, I suddenly had the strength of a lion. I stood up, looked him square in the eye, and said, "WEAK! Is that what you think it was all about? Let me tell you, John Avient, if you had to go through what I have gone through, you would be dead now because you would have taken a gun and blown your bloody head off! I survived because I have strength, the likes of which you have never known. And don't you ever forget that!!" He never has.

As you know, I had been working at the lab in Sherwood Park at the time of my breakdown and the time had come for me to return to work. I was dreading that with a passion. Formerly, I had been very good at my work, but for the most part it was boring; the only time it got interesting was at the expense of someone else. For lab techs to get excited, a patient has to be very, very sick. I hated that. I also felt there was not much of a sense of accomplishment in this work because to me it was work that anyone could do. To understand the medical theories behind the tests we performed takes a little training, but the tests themselves could have been done by anybody.

I only lasted back at work for a few months when I was asked to resign. I was told that the other workers had complained about me because they felt that I was not doing very well at my job. Apparently the technicians who had been working with me when I was in charge of the lab were assigned to check all of my work. I was just plain insulted. My pride was hurt because essentially I was fired; on another level, however, I was singing, "Hallelujah"!

Around this same time, I began a part of my life that would prove unprofitable as far as money was concerned, but invaluable as a means of learning a lot about me; not all that I learned was good. I became an Avon representative.

Right from the beginning, Verna, my Avon manager, gave up trying to train me, because every time she tried to get me to role play as though I was talking to a customer, I would go into my fear mode and my throat would close up. I was not afraid of talking to the customer, I was afraid of failing the "test" that Verna was putting me through. To my relief, one day she told me to just go out and do it. I inquired as to the highest amount that any of her salespeople had sold in a three-week sales campaign. She said, "$1200." When I heard that amount, I knew she was really saying, "$1200, and that is what I expect from you." She had not said that, but that is what I heard. So off I went to find some customers.

On my first run through my sales territory, no one would talk to me, and I had doors slammed in my face, so to speak. I decided to personalize my approach so I wrote my first of many sales letters telling the would-be clients about me, my family, and about the fabulous products for sale in that campaign's brochure. I delivered them the next day and the sales began. In my first campaign, I sold $1400 and nearly caused my manager to have a coronary.

Over the next 18 months, I developed a vast client base and did things that most Avon salespeople do not do. Within the first six months, I was the top salesperson in our area of 200 and 10th in the district of 4000 sales personnel. My customers loved me and, more importantly, they trusted me. I merely had to recommend a product and I could consider it sold because, when necessary, I also told them what products to stay away from. The district sales manager came to town and took me out for dinner; she wanted to know how I was doing it. She then asked me to make a tape for her to use at the next national sales conference. I did and I felt important for a time.

From the outside my life was looking up, but on the inside some weird and wacky things were going on. I had been having a tough time finding an antidepressant that would actually work, so the doctor finally put me on a drug that had just come on the market called Nadir. (Note: this is not its real name.) He also put me on a sleeping pill that I believe became very controversial in later years, but I will not name it in case I am mistaken. Anyway, I do know that the name began with an *H*.

In the beginning, until the correct dosage was obtained, Nadir had a very strange effect on me. It made me laugh hysterically about anything and everything. Sean said that he would rather see me in a deep depression any day than to have to live with that malicious laughter. That may sound strange and even dramatic, but the laughter was offensive and totally inappropriate. I could hear myself doing it, but I had no power to stop it. One of the most horrible experiences of our lives occurred during this period.

Nadir brought out the evil side of me, the side that no one thinks he or she has. I can say with all certainty that I did not know I had one until this particular night. I had always seen myself as a kind and caring person who would not hurt any living thing. Sean, Jason, and I were just finishing up the dishes on about the fifth day of me taking my new antidepressant. All of a sudden, I lay down on the kitchen floor in a sprawled-out position. The kids asked me what I was doing. I said, in a voice that haunts me still, that this was how they were going to find me one day. I chortled and said that I could easily kill myself, and assured my two sweet boys that someday very soon I would do just that. My suicide had been a constant fear for them, and here I was making light of it and threatening them with it.

Then more laughter set in and my imagination went into

overdrive, fed by the fear and outright horror that I could see in their eyes. I went on to tell them that the police would probably have to put a chalk mark around my body so that they would know where I had been lying. The chalk mark would settle into the rug so, no matter where they were in the kitchen, in years to come they would have the reminder of me there right before their eyes. (It never even occurred to me that they would move out of the house if this happened.)

Sean begged me to stop talking like that and I could see the tears welling up in his eyes. That reaction just stoked the fire that was building inside of me. The more they cried, the more I laughed or, shall I say, the more I cackled. I do not know how long the scene lasted, but it seemed like forever. I am sure it seemed longer than that to the boys.

On another occasion, I hurt my brother, David, very badly. We were playing cards with him and his wife, Pat, when I suddenly starting screaming at him. I hollered at him that he was probably going to be just as nuts as I was one day and that he deserved it. I went on and on until I had my dear brother in tears. Believe me, that was completely out of character for him. John dragged me out the door and told me how ashamed he was of me. To that, I flippantly replied, "Oh well. At least *I* feel better."

Finally, the Nadir incidents ended. I did not know the damage I had done until much, much later when the correct dosage was found. I told my doctor what I had done to my sons and he told me that I was a cruel and abusive mother. He did not care why I had done it or what had caused it. He did not even consider that perhaps the pills had brought my mania— that he had diagnosed me as having—to the surface with a vengeance. Nothing more was said. He just gave me some more pills and sent me home. (In 2003, a doctor told me that antidepressants actually increase the magnitude of manic episodes and that Nadir obviously was one that triggered the most mania in me.)

After that, because of what the doctor had said, I went on a mission to punish myself. I had all the tools I needed right there in my home. First of all, I had a very clever, very sick mind and lots of pills. At that time I was taking Lithium, Nadir, and sleeping pills; between them I swallowed over a dozen pills each day. I also began collecting a stash of pills for the day when I decided that I could not bear to live anymore. In the meantime, I decided that I would have to suffer for the pain I had caused the boys, John, and my brother. I am sure that I came up with all sorts of other ills that I had perpetrated on my mother and other family members. In retaliation to my bad actions, I gave up sleeping, resting, and all means of comfort to my body.

I started going to bed on the floor at night; first with a pillow and a blanket, and when that became too comfortable, I got rid of the pillow and just laid on the floor. Then I decided that a person like me deserved much less than that, so I started looking at other comfortable things in my life that could be eliminated.

I would not allow myself to sit on a cushioned chair of any kind. I prescribed myself to sit only on wooden chairs and stuck to that for many months. I did not let myself go into the living room because of the comfortable chairs in there, so John brought an armchair into our kitchen and put it in front of the television set there. That way he could at least be in the same room with me. Luckily we had a kitchen that was as large as most living rooms so unfortunately this did not really inconvenience us. Why do I say that it was unfortunate? Because we *could* do it, we *did* do it. In effect, it encouraged my bizarre behavior. If it had been a hardship or a total inconvenience, then maybe someone would have questioned it. We did not know anyone else who had a big armchair in the middle of the kitchen—for that matter, we did not know anyone with a kitchen as big as ours! Even the doctor did not question this, and he knew about it because when I went to his office, I insisted on sitting on a wooden chair rather than letting myself be comfortable in his plush leather ones.

Then I stopped going to bed at all. As you can imagine, I got very, very tired after a few days of this. On one memorable evening, I knelt on the floor at the end of my bed and put my head on the bed. I told myself that this was all right because my *body* was not resting; I convinced myself that I would not go to sleep. Predictably, I did doze off, and the boys found me. I awoke to feeling them trying to lift me very gently up onto the bed. When I realized what they were doing, I went crazy shouting and yelling at them to stop. I went up one side of them and down the other chastising them for going against my wishes. I recall saying to them, "How dare you try to trick me into going to bed! You know I can't let myself go to sleep. Don't you ever do this again!" I would not believe them when they said that I really had been sleeping. I was not to be reasoned with; they both had to put up with my wrath for the rest of "just another zany day in the Avient household." The craziest thing was that I was not even slightly concerned about the quality of our lives.

My favorite place became my wooden chair at the wooden kitchen table. I sat there every night working on Avon ideas and making lists, and lists, and more lists of things to do. I was obsessed. The funny thing about that obsession was that to my family, I was behaving very weird and slightly insane, but to my customers I was perceived as "remarkable and totally together." They had no idea of the Hell that went on at home.

That was when I discovered another character inside of me. I simply called her "The Avon Lady." I was a walking, talking maniac at home, but every morning I got dressed, put on my special prim and proper Avon Lady earrings, and went out to sell, sell, sell. I could hear myself talking to my customers, but I was not doing the talking. One time in 1986, when I (or so it would seem) was telling a client that I had to go into hospital, I remember swearing and cussing at this prissy saleslady who was using my body and talking through me. Here "I" was telling this woman that I am going into hospital for depression and she says that she had never even seen me looking like I was feeling down. I stood there swearing at the Avon Lady in my mind because she had so misrepresented us to all these people.

One might think that the Avon Lady was similar to the work side of ourselves that we all show to the rest of the world, but this was not the case. I referred to her in the third person and I was always talking to her in my mind while she was conversing with or selling to anyone. There were definitely two people standing in front of all of our customers. The Avon Lady was so serene, so confident, so smiling, and so unlike the "me" that was at home or who had been in hospital. I had a method of telling which personality was out—by the earrings on my ears. Lulubelle wore big huge hoop earrings and The Avon Lady wore "Miss Goodie Two Shoes" jewelry. That is how I also know that these were two other distinct personalities in me; I hated them both and I let them know it, but I could not function in this world without them.

During the months of not sleeping in my bed, I did find a way to get a little bit of rest. I took my sleeping pill every night, because the doctor told me to take it; I would just choose not to go to bed. I usually did not take the pill until about 4 or 5 am (I remember seeing many sunrises). Because I would not go to bed, I was forced to fall asleep at the table. On far too many mornings, the boys found me on the floor in the kitchen, asleep—not dead. It became a part of their morning ritual to prop their mother up in her chair from off the floor before going to school each day.

Whenever I took a sleeping pill, I experienced an instant affinity for sweets. Many mornings at home, and later in hospital, I would be found with chocolate smeared all over my face, squished in my hand, or stuck to my clothing.

[I do not remember the exact timing of some things, because with all my medication and lack of sleep, I have lost sequential memory for this period of my life. I do not remember events in relation to other events. I just remember a whole lot of isolated situations that happened one by one. The events that were exacerbated by my pills are examples of this.]

Another negative effect of taking Nadir was that I fell asleep spontaneously and at very inopportune times. To get to our home at South Cooking Lake, I had to travel on a highway that was divided until the last couple of kilometers. At the point when it turned into a two-way road, the outside lane just merged into the other one as it went around a bend. One day while driving home, I fell asleep right at the point where the road turned and the lanes merged into one; the road turned but I did not go with it. I kept driving straight and went off the road down into the ditch. I did manage to wake up before anything serious happened. As I came to, I could hear long grass swishing along the bottom of the vehicle. My foot was still heavily on the gas so my car was trying to drive fast, but the tall grass was slowing me down considerably. I was more concerned about whether anyone else had seen me do this crazy thing than worrying about whether or not I was hurt. As far as I can remember, I did not try to slow the car down; I just drove up the nearest embankment, up onto the road, and continued on home. I did not tell anyone that it had happened until much, much later.

Then I started falling asleep in other situations. In the middle of a meal, my head would just fall into my plate. I badly bruised my nose one morning on my cereal bowl. An hour later, I went to see an Avon customer and I fell asleep while talking to her. She just let me sleep. I was astounded and embarrassed. She was really great about it, but I am sure that she thought it was very strange.

By the time I started spontaneously falling asleep, I was out of the period in which I refused to rest or sit in comfortable chairs. It just seemed as though I flitted from one problematic phase to another.

I remember one night when John took me out to dinner at the restaurant overlooking the racetrack in Edmonton. We usually did this once a year and enjoyed picking winners while eating a good meal. Not so enjoyable that particular night! In front of all the other patrons, my head fell onto the table as I fell sound asleep. I am sure everyone thought I was drunk and poor John was totally mortified. I had a cigarette in my hand and burned a hole in my dress. In fact, in those days I did this so often that every item of clothing I owned had burn holes in it. After that night, John stopped taking me out.

Marilyn Avient

CHAPTER 11

In 1986, I felt myself going completely out of control again. My bouts of sadness were overwhelming and my thoughts of suicide were becoming a little more real to me. I asked the doctor to please put me back into the hospital and he did—for another six weeks. I guess I must have been showing more signs that I wanted to hurt myself than during the last visit because this time they were taking me seriously. Perhaps just the fact that it was my second visit put more validity to my references to being tired of living.

I was immediately put on suicide watch. I absolutely loved this. It meant that every 15 minutes one of the nurses would inquire as to how I was feeling. For the first time in my life, someone was keeping an eye on me. I pretended it was because they really cared. When I was a girl in school, I would study every night in my room, and I always wished that once in a while, someone would knock on the door and ask if I was all right. No one ever did. I know it was only because Mom and Dad did not want to disturb me, but it would have been nice anyway. At this point in my life, being fragile was having a payoff and I wished that the attention could go on forever.

My friend Beth, who had been constantly there for me during my first stay in hospital, gave up on me when I went in the second time. She was a person who liked to rescue and heal others, and when she saw that I was not ready for either of those two things, she gave up on me. I remember sitting in the large common room one afternoon when I saw her going up to the desk at the nursing station. I was so happy that she had come to visit me, but then I saw her hand the nurse a large manila envelope and walk away. The nurse brought me the envelope and when I opened it I found the longest letter I had ever seen. In her "epic" *my friend* ripped me apart limb by limb; I do not remember ever being hurt by anything as much as I was by her words that day. I was so upset that the nurses took me to see my therapist and somehow he managed to make me feel better—at least as better as was possible under the circumstances.

As much as I did not deserve the things she said, I went crawling back to her with my tail between my legs as soon as I got out. Beth always had a way of cloaking "my way or the highway" under the guise of friendship. I then spent the next months literally sucking up to her as I tried to get back in her favor. It only worked for a while. She deserted me again when I went into hospital the third time. Again, I went crawling back to her and our "friendship" resumed for many years . . . then it just slowly withered away as both our lives changed. Relationships come into our lives for a reason; when the reason dies, so does the relationship.

I was obsessed with selling Avon when I went into hospital this time and Sean became the brunt of that extreme focus. I told him that he had to take over for me while I was away. When the Avon order came in, I wanted him to sort it and then deliver the goods. Now this was on top of him being in charge of the house, going to school, taking care of Jason, and anything else that came along. He was 17 at this time so I did not think that I was asking too much—if the truth be known

I was so into "I am queen of the world" mode that I did not consider for one minute what I was doing to my own son.

One night he called me at the hospital and he was very upset. He told me that he just could not handle the Avon and this made me absolutely livid. There I stood in the middle of the ward screeching like a mad woman out of control. My doctor heard about my tirade and raked me over the coals. He told me that I was a terrible mother who should be shot and that if I did not be careful, Sean would end up in hospital as well. That seemed to snap me into awareness. I called Sean and apologized. After thinking for a couple of days I wrote him a letter telling him that he was not responsible for me or my life. My apology was sincere, but as Sean had been in the role of being my caretaker for all his life, neither of us really knew what to do to change the status quo of our relationship. Actually, it took until 1989 for him to even begin to slip my noose off his neck.

The second stay in hospital was quiet different from the first. This time, I was a veteran and I was immediately accepted into the group. I knew I had made it when one of the real old-timers took me aside and told me that if I ever wanted to "off" myself, to let her know, because she had ways to get the pills that do the job the fastest and the most efficiently. I told her I would keep that in mind. It seemed very normal to be talking in that way; I should have been scared about that, but I was not. Instead, I felt accepted. I also felt relieved and safe because someone believed and understood me.

I remember one particularly low day that involved a session in a huge Jacuzzi pool. I was still on suicide watch because I recall being escorted to and from the pool by a nurse who presented me with a bathing suit and then told me to follow her. She said it was time for some pool therapy. I told her I was afraid of water and did not want to go, but she just ignored my pleas.

The therapist in charge of the water activities told me that I could just sit on the stairs if I was frightened. I appreciated his understanding my fear, which was much more than a small problem—I was terrified. Relieved to get a respite of sorts, I sat and behaved myself. Before long, I was mesmerized by bubbles that resulted from the constantly swirling water. I found myself identifying with those bubbles and thinking that I felt like they looked—forced to move around with no minds of their own while waiting to fall to the bottom at any moment. My eyes then slipped down farther to a point far below the bubbles and I saw such absolute serenity that I had to hang on to the railing to keep myself from falling in so I could become one with that calm. I was hanging on so tight, tears streaming down my face, that the therapist came over to help me. He thought that I was terrified of the water and I wanted out. He was shocked when I said I was trying to keep myself from falling in because I wanted to go to that peaceful place under the bubbles. He said I had to go back to my room and he called for my nurse to come get me.

The nurse took me back all right, but when I got to my room I was met by a doctor and two nurses who wanted to know everything that had happened to me at the pool. After I told them, they concluded that I wanted to drown myself; I just shrugged my shoulders and I told them that all I wanted to do was to get to that quiet place below the bubbles.

One of the women whom I had come to know was moving into an apartment, but she had no household furnishings. On my weekends at home, I packed up boxes of items and, before long, I had literally created a home for her. I think we even gave her a couch, and why not? I gave her everything else she could possibly need. All in all, we took more than two full truckloads to her place the day she moved in. She was shocked at my generosity. I felt then that I really was one of the gang! In later months when I went to visit her, it was like going home, because most of what she owned had been mine. This gift to her was only partly out of kindness; actually, it was just another subconscious ploy to get someone to love and accept me. I wanted to be a hero to someone!

Then there was another female patient who literally had only the clothes on her back, so I went through my closet and brought her six big bags of clothes. She could not believe it and, again, I felt good because I had bought someone's affection. I knew I had found a method that worked for making friends.

Not long after that, I was down in the occupational therapy department and I saw that they did many of the crafts that I had done at home. The only difference was that I had more supplies than they did, so that department of the hospital became my next project. I brought in dozens and dozens of balls of twine for macramé and was actually feeling quite good with myself.

Within an hour of presenting the twine to the occupational therapist, I had two nurses and a doctor descend upon me in my room—just like the last time. They were looking so very serious that I asked them what I had done. They told me that when a person starts giving away all his or her belongings, it is a sure sign that he or she is planning to commit suicide very soon. I tried to tell them that I just liked to give stuff away because it made me feel good and people liked me for it; they would not listen. I cannot imagine what they would have done with me if they found out about the apartment I furnished or the wardrobe I had provided for the two girls on the ward.

I was told that I was on an upgraded suicide watch and would not be able to go out on any more passes because I was more seriously ill than they had previously thought. They also warned that this time further treatment might have to be implemented if anything like this happened again. I knew that they were considering electric shock treatments, so I simply decided that I would have to be more careful about what I said and did from then on.

Shortly thereafter, I was asked if I would be willing to go into deep therapy. When I asked what that entailed, I was told that I would meet with a psychologist on a regular basis and with his help I would delve into my past and into the hidden parts of my mind. I remember being warned that it would take much courage. I surprised myself by immediately saying that I definitely wanted to go this route; I thus met a man named Ivan.

I was immediately attracted to this man who came to escort me from the ward to his office for my first visit. While waiting for the elevator, he asked me how I was—as people commonly do when they meet. I heard my mouth answer something to the effect of "Who the f---cares?" I could not believe my ears. My first thought was that Lulubelle was back and she was angry that I had shut her out for so long. He merely shrugged, and when we got to his office he said something else, to which I had a meek and mild little answer that, I definitely knew, came from "me." When he heard my reply to his second query, he looked at me, and said, "So who was I talking to at the elevator?" I burst out crying because I knew that finally someone was willing to see what no one else had seen before. That day I began the long journey to get to know the girl behind the closed door.

There is a thing called transference in the world of

psychiatry and I experienced it. I mistakenly interpreted Ivan's professional astuteness, coupled with his good looks and kindness, and I fell head over heels "in love" with him. Nobody had ever treated me the way he did, because he acknowledged all sides of me. He made me feel "not crazy." He accepted me and all my *pals* as normal, and because he was willing to listen without judgment, I was able to talk about them and everything else in my life with freedom. He let me talk about my dad in ways that I had never been able to before. I felt safe.

When I left the hospital, I cried about leaving Ivan. I needed his care to survive, because only with him did I feel safe. After being home for a week, I went to his office and told him how strongly I felt about him. He said that he was very flattered, but it was against his professional ethics to do anything about it. As I was leaving, he hugged me good-bye and then he kissed me. I almost succumbed right there on the spot—this was no kiss on the cheek; it was a long and lingering kiss on the mouth. After that, I really began to miss him. When I next saw him, I told him that nothing had changed and I had been very upset and confused over the kiss. He again told me that he was flattered and that nothing could come of these feelings. When we were done talking, I saw that he was looking at me strangely; I asked him what was wrong. He replied, "Nothing is wrong. I am just wondering how I am going to let you get out the door without kissing you again." I smiled and left, feeling a victory of sorts.

Weeks later, after calmly telling my poor husband about my attraction for Ivan, I decided to go through some old photographs. I came across a studio photo of my father when he was in his late teens. He was wearing a newsboy-style hat and he looked very mature and very handsome. I had seen this picture many times before, but it had never affected me like this. As soon as my eyes landed on it, I screamed and began to sob; I acted very much like the unhinged person that I professed to be. I did not see my dad in this picture this time; I saw Ivan. I had not fallen for him—I had fallen for my dad. That is who Ivan reminded me of; I had never noticed the resemblance on a conscious level. I immediately phoned Ivan and told him about my findings. He said he was glad that I had figured it out.

I saw Ivan again the next time I was in hospital and he outwardly flirted with me. By that time I was angry at him, and told the nurses about him, but they were protective of their own and told me that I was imagining things. Why was I angry when I was the one who had made the overtures of affection? I was angry because he was the professional and I was a sick woman medicated up to the eyeballs. He had said that he was *flattered* by my attraction to him, instead of explaining to me that this happens frequently between patients and doctors for the very reasons that I was attracted to him. In some ways I was still attracted to him because he was the only one who had believed me, he had validated my feelings, and if nothing else, he had listened to me. Who would *not* fall in love with a man who did all that? I was sure that John did not love me, so I was a perfect candidate for this phenomenon called *transference*.

About ten years later, I was driving down Whyte Avenue in Edmonton around lunchtime, and I literally almost ran over Ivan in a crosswalk. I was shocked to see him; another foot closer and he would have gone splat all over the front of my car—talk about a bittersweet thought! I quickly turned the corner, parked my car, and followed him into a restaurant. He failed to recognize me at first, but when I told him my name, I could see him shudder for a moment, and then I saw admiration. I was glad that I had curled my hair and bothered to put on makeup that day. I told him once again how embarrassed I was to have said the things that I had said all those years before. I told Ivan that I had done some work with another therapist and my supposed attraction to him now made perfect sense; I had not been attracted to him at all in reality. I felt strong; he looked sheepish. Then I pulled a trick on him because I wanted to know where he was working, in case I wanted to take any further action against him.

I told him that perhaps a session or two would be helpful to really resolve this issue and I asked him for his business card. He gave it to me. Over the next 24 hours I got more and more angry at him; by so recklessly handling my affections, he mistreated the child in me; he led me on when he knew exactly what was going on, even if I did not. I decided to have a talk with God, and this is what I said, "God, I am feeling such anger, within me, towards this man named Ivan. He let me feel things many years ago that were a result of my illness and my vulnerability. He was a professional who should have nipped it in the bud. I need to tell him how he hurt the child that was me, the child who felt so safe that she thought she loved him. I will make a deal with you. I am going to his office tomorrow, and if he is there, and if he is available for me to talk to, then I will say all that is on my mind and I will know that you want me to do this. However, if he is not there, I will know that you do not deem it necessary to think about this anymore and I will let it go. I promise."

I went to his office and he was not there. When his partner told me that he was out for lunch at the time, I thanked him and walked away. I felt the anger drain out of me like water from a tap. True to my word, I never thought of it again, until I decided to include it in this writing.

After getting out of hospital the second time around, in November 1986, I felt more lost than after the first stay. That was probably because I did not have anything planned, such as day therapy, and I did not have a job to go back to. I had no idea what I was living for at all. The months following my release are blank . . . except for one disturbing memory.

Sean started dating the woman destined to be his wife, Janet, in February 1987 and during their courtship, one particular evening stands out for me. I was in the den writing a story and thought that I was feeling pretty good. Sean must have thought so too, as he came into the den dressed up in a smart-looking sports jacket and dress pants. Being a joker, he sidled into the room holding his lapels and said, "Hey, Ma, would you take a look at Sean tonight! Lookin' *fine!*" My reaction caught us both by surprise!

I nearly jumped over the desk in anger, grabbed him by his jacket sleeve, and dragged him into the dining room. This was no easy feat because he was about six feet tall at that time. He could have stopped me but he would never have raised a hand to me—his loving mother! When we got to the dining room I pointed at my favorite picture of him as a small child and said in a caustic, accusatory voice, "*You* are not Sean—*this* is Sean and don't you ever say that to me again." I dismissed him with a flick of my hand, left the room, and went back to my writing. No sense; no reason; just cruel insanity.

CHAPTER 12

Throughout this book so far, you have heard a myriad of references to my elder son, Sean. He is the easy one to include because his role was so paramount during my "sick years." So what about Jason? During the years of my being in and out of hospital, Jason had his own trauma that he was going through. I, as his mother, cannot tell my own story without including his. After reading the unedited version of this chapter, Jason asked if he could give a short narrative to provide some first-hand insights into his condition.

Obsessive-compulsive disorder (OCD) is a common mental health challenge in North America that is clinically caused by low levels of serotonin in the bloodstream (Ironically, clinical depression has the same cause.) A person with OCD experiences "obsessions" that can range from, but are hardly limited to, personal hygiene and cleanliness; to the safety of oneself and one's family; to perceived moral or ethical obligations. For me, my obsessions mostly revolved around what I felt was right or wrong and, in general, about just being a good person. I would have thoughts like "If I brush my teeth perfectly I will go to heaven" or "If I make a mistake I'll go to Hell." The obsessions can take over a person's life. To reduce the stress caused by these thoughts, someone with OCD is compelled to undertake what, to someone else, would seem like strange rituals. For me, some of the rituals included drying my hands one finger at a time in a certain pattern;

brushing my teeth in a certain way and starting over if the pattern was done less than perfectly; folding the dishcloth precisely after doing the dishes even if it meant spending an hour to get it that way; kneeling rigidly for long periods while praying about anything and everything, all the while feeling I could not stop until the whole gamut of issues had been covered.

What is interesting about this disorder is that friends, family, and colleagues of someone with OCD often never know that he or she has it. One reason is because a person with OCD knows the obsessions and compulsions make no sense, so that person tries to hide them out of embarrassment. This is a double-edged sword. On one hand, it took three years to get help because I did not let anyone see that I needed it. On the other, my family felt like they had failed me: "How could we not have known something was wrong?" Well, that was easy—I was a good actor, and I lied a lot when they asked me about the odd behavior they had seen.

Jason was an adorable child. Everybody commented on how nice it was to have him around with his good looks, his placid temperament, and delightful way of endearing himself to everyone. After his father Dan and I separated, Jason became very close to Sean. People who say that toddlers are not affected by divorce should have watched Jason at that time. The only person he trusted was Sean and he stuck to him like glue. I am not exaggerating when I say that it was as though the two of them became one.

However, once the school years began, Jason became much more outgoing than his brother. When he was in grade 1, he would come in from school and tell me about all the little girls who had walked home with him. He would say, "Mommy, they all just love me." Of course I would smile at him and tell him that I didn't blame them. His mannerisms and faith in himself around these children were not in the least bit arrogant. He was just one of those children who are almost angelic in their nature. Don't misunderstand me; he had less attractive traits too—like being stubborn to a fault—but most of all he was pretty easy to be around.

I got married to my present husband John in March 1977 and by November 1978 he had completed our beautiful home at South Cooking Lake. Jason was in grade 3 when we moved in. The move was very hard on him because he had so many friends at his old school; it took a while for him to settle in with new friends and new teachers. However, he managed very well. As the years went by his cheerfulness and hardworking study habits made him popular with students and teachers alike. Looking back, I wish that I had not taken Jason's sunny personality for granted in those years because, unbeknown to me, it was not going to last forever.

Jason's 15th birthday in November 1985, during his first year in high school, was a happy one for him. About a dozen of his closest friends paid for a "Scheme a Dream" clown to come all the way out to their school in the country to present him with a bouquet of balloons. Then they threw him a surprise birthday party as well. He was a popular lad—if he had known what was coming, perhaps he would have appreciated it more.

Sometime during the months that followed, we began to see changes in Jason. The first memorable sign that something was different with him occurred frequently after school. Jason would go into the washroom and stay there for what seemed like hours at a time. I would call to him to see if he was all right and he always said he was. We had many talks in those months—you know the kind, where the parent asks the questions and the child gives few, if any, answers. This was so unlike him, and I am sure that more than a little of this behavior was put down to the fact that he was going through the upheavals of being a teenager.

Sometimes that explanation placated me, but Jason's new behavior nagged at me. One day, before too long, I did not have to wonder anymore because I saw without a doubt that everything was wrong in my dear son's world. *And remember that this is the same time when I was doing very zany things; there was a lot going on in that lovely house out in the country that no one on the outside had any idea about.*

On that day, I sent Sean to get his brother because dinner was ready. The next thing I heard was Sean yelling for me to come to Jason's room. I ran to his room and there I saw Jason on his knees by his bed. He was praying out loud, talking very fast, and all the while tears were streaming down his face. In his hand he was clutching—for all he was worth—a cross that he had made out of cardboard and covered with tinfoil. He had been in a play at school about a monastery and he had used the cross while playing the part of one the monks.

I immediately tried to take him in my arms, but he told me that if he stopped praying, he was afraid that the devil would possess him. I could hardly believe what he had said because although we were not a practicing religious family, we had no room in our lives for any form of evil either. The boys had never shown any interest in watching movies with any kind of satanic theme and if they had, I would have denied them the privilege. At the moment of his declaration, I went cold. I knew that the Jason I had known was gone.

That night was a long one. Jason would not talk to me other than to keep repeating that he was afraid the devil would possess him if he did not rid himself of his sins. The very next morning I got him an appointment with a psychiatrist. Basically the doctor said that Jason was depressed, put him on some pills, and sent us home. Jason took the pills, but they did nothing. I instinctively knew he was not suffering only from depression, but doctors are gods, so who was I to argue?

Somehow he got through the following months without his grades suffering too much. This is very unusual, I was later told, because depressed students frequently have trouble doing the required schoolwork, so their grades fall. The schedule he set for himself was painful to watch. He would come in from school around 4 pm, sometimes do the bathroom routine, which was now down to an hour or two, and then study until late into the night. No matter how much I prodded him, he would not stop. When he did, he still needed to spend an hour praying.

I later found out that the bathroom routine was a mixture of praying and washing his hands, which sometimes had to be repeated many times until he felt that they were satisfactory. He had to pay heed to his obsessive thoughts because failing to do so would result in a threat to his life or the life of one of his family. He also had to brush his teeth over and over again until the compulsion had passed and he let himself stop. This routine was dreaded by him, but it went on day in and day out. The silver lining to all that brushing was that he now has the best looking teeth on the planet!

By May of 1986, I had spoken to Jason's counselor and all his teachers at school about his condition. They had all noticed a severe change in him, but had not known what was going on at all. He was so exhausted by mid-May that I got special permission from the school to let him finish his school term at that time. They gave him good grades in all of his classes and continued without him.

After seeing the first psychiatrist for all those months, I still doubted the validity of his diagnosis. Unfortunately for Jason, I was still battling my own demons, and I ended up in hospital again in September of that same year. While there, my own doctor recommended that I take Jason to a child psychiatrist who was new to the city. Getting a pass from the hospital, I took my son to see this man, who immediately diagnosed him with OCD and changed his medications. Believe it or not, he was put on Nadir, which was the medication that caused such havoc for me. Because Jason was not bipolar, it did not have the same effect on him. But knowing what he had and curing this condition were two entirely different things. As soon as we knew what it was, the symptoms somehow seemed to escalate in intensity.

When I took Jason to this doctor I was in fragile shape myself and as you know I having a hard time handling the world as it was. I thought things could not get any worse, but I was wrong. This doctor proclaimed when he heard that I was bipolar, "It all makes sense to me now. Bipolar mothers often give birth to children with OCD." Now it sounded like it was my fault that my sweet son was suffering as he was. I had difficulty wrestling with the guilt of that for many years.

By this time, Jason had gone back to school for his 11th year. Once again, the study schedule became unbearable—from after school until late into the night, and even more on Saturday and Sunday. I told him he did not have to carry on with this outrageous work load, but he said that he did. I did not argue because I knew that to do so would be futile; he was obviously dealing actively with the exhausting thoughts that were now just a natural part of his life.

As the self-perpetuated demands in his head escalated, the effects became more noticeable in his appearance and he looked tired all of the time. At school, his friends were disappearing with such velocity that on his 16th birthday—only one year after the huge party of the previous year—he received just one card from the two friends who were the last to leave him. One of those friends was a girl named Laura whose mother I had gotten to know through selling Avon. I was driving down the highway going home one afternoon and I heard a little voice telling me to go to Laura's house. The turn to their place was coming up soon but I really did not want to go, so I ignored it. I was almost at their road and again I was told to go. I still resisted, but it was as though the car turned all by itself and before I knew it I was heading down the road to see Laura's mother. When I got to her door, I felt silly. She answered the doorbell and stood there looking at me with astonishment on her face. I said that I did not know why I was there and she said, "When the doorbell rang I was in the middle of a prayer asking for help as to whether I should call you or not." She went on, "Laura told me last night that many of the kids at school are worried about Jason and so he has been reported to the Peer Support Group as a possible suicide risk." I was upset by the news but relieved at the same time because at least I knew now that someone was watching out for my Jason at school. After thanking her, I headed for home. On the way I thanked God for making me head down that road, even when I did not want to. I saw it as a miracle.

In spite of that concern, his friends were young and youth is not known for its sensitivity to anything out of the norm. Apparently, Jason occasionally spent a large chunk of time in the washroom at school. To their young minds, this meant only one of two things: he was doing drugs or he was having sexual problems. Neither one was true. He had to spend all that time in the washroom because that was the only place at school where he could pray. His friend Laura told me that whenever Jason was asked a question, he would take an unusually long time to answer. Apparently, he had to do a mental check on all the possible words that his compulsive self would allow him to use as an answer. So their immediate questions would be met with silence and then what seemed like minutes later he would respond very quietly. Of course by that time, they had given up on him and had gone on to talk about other things. Soon they just stopped talking to him at all.

The students also found it strange that Jason slept through every French class and no one, not even the teacher, who was usually so strict, tried to wake him. Somehow he passed French and all his other subjects that year. The teachers said that although they knew he was very ill, his work was still of amazingly high caliber.

At home, we were bombarded with just as much uncharacteristic behavior. One Sunday, after studying many, many hours on Saturday, Jason came to me in a panic. He had five big assignments due on Monday and he did not know where to begin. I realized then that although he put in long hours, he did not accomplish much. I told him to do one assignment at a time and that if he failed to get something done, his teachers were all aware of what was happening with him. So he sat down and prepared to write an essay. He was using a legal-size pad and had just completed one full page in the tiniest writing that you have ever seen when he became overwhelmed with thoughts that forced him to do it again or I, his mother, would be killed. When I checked in on him later, he was on the third rewriting by hand of the same paper and the tears were flowing in a sad continual stream down his face. My heart broke for him, but because my life had been threatened, he had to keep at it. In all, he kept rewriting that same paper over and over for hours on end.

Another day, I found him on his knees holding his cross in front of the open refrigerator. He was praying with much fervor because he believed that until he did so he could not eat. When he saw Sean cooking some soup for us, he irrationally told himself that he could not eat it because his brother and I were trying to poison him. Much to my dismay, Jason ate nothing at all that day.

Whenever Jason would help out with any household chores—which was not that often because he had so many rituals to perform while doing anything—it would be painful to watch. If he went to wipe off the counter with the dishcloth, he would have to count the number of times he wrung out the cloth and then he would have to fold it perfectly on the first try. If, for example, one corner hung over the other just a little on the first fold, then he would have to put it back in the water, wring it out the required number of times and then try to refold it once more. I painfully watched him go through this about ten times one day.

When Jason dried his hands he had a ritual of drying each finger a set number of times. If he lost count or did a finger out of order, he had to wash his hands again and then repeat the whole drying procedure. When he got his driver's license, he had to wait until his thoughts gave him the go-ahead signal to start his car. Often he would sit there and pray as he waited. I have seen him wait 10 or 15 minutes before driving away. One time when he was driving me in my car, he pulled over and told me that I would have to drive the rest of the way. He said that he felt an almost overwhelming compulsion to kill us both by driving over the embankment and into the deep ditch that ran along the side of the road. Although I was upset by this, I also felt a glimmer of hope, because it was the first time that he had stood up to himself, and he was surprised when the "urge to harm" actually subsided.

The doctor had been telling Jason for weeks that if the obsessive and compulsive behavior did not lessen, he would have to be hospitalized to receive massive doses of medication to drastically increase his serotonin levels. Jason had seen enough of hospitals through visiting me, so he was very afraid of it. I could not understand his fear, because I found the hospital to be literally a lifesaver and not an unpleasant place at all. He refused to go, but finally agreed that if he was still in the same shape by the summer of that year, he would do as the doctor wanted. In the meantime, the current therapy continued and he and I kept on talking. In a way, my own problems helped with his, because I could see him differently than some other people did. I knew what mental pain felt like and somehow I would just have to wait him out.

One thing that finally helped pull Jason back (probably after the medication started to kick in) was the knowledge that the thoughts were of his own making. He slowly began to reason that because he could see they were not there for anyone else, they must belong solely to him. It took a while for him to totally believe this, but finally he concluded that if he created the thoughts, he could also destroy them. Soon after this line of thinking came into play, the resulting strange behavior began to lessen somewhat. By the summer of that year, he had progressed enough that the doctor said hospitalization was no longer necessary.

I was very happy to see the horrors of his condition lessen to a large degree. Daily, I waited for my son Jason to reappear. The person who stood in his place was a very lovable and very loving person, but he was not the same. Who knows, maybe he was better than he would have been if he had never gone through it all. The firsthand knowledge of pain is a powerful

Marilyn Avient

teacher, but the innocence lost in the process was pitiful in nature and magnanimous in volume.

Although I tried to bolster his spirits by telling him that he had emerged a victor, I do not think Jason felt that way at all. He said he did not care that some people with OCD never make it out. Jason was not being unkind; he was just sad. He went through grade 12 all alone; his friends never came back. He did not have a date for the graduation dance and banquet. At the award ceremonies that took place the following September, he broke my heart as he cried much of the way home. He said he could not believe that he had finished school without one friend to his name. At that moment, I felt the OCD had killed him and I think he felt the same.

I feel like a traitor saying that the son who came out of OCD is still not the same one who went in, but for me it is true. Sometimes I have felt like a mother whose son died, and we never got to say good-bye. Then I look at the strong young man who stands before me and I thank God and all the angels for this new gift that I have been given. He is a wonderful, kind, and giving person and I feel truly blessed. One day not too long ago, after an exceptionally quiet time, Jason said something witty. He startled me because I heard a tone in his voice that I had not heard for many, many years. I looked up. Jason's eyes were sparkling for just a moment but long enough for me to see Jason, my little boy. Finally, the wait is over. Now I know that Jason the child is still alive inside Jason the man. I know he is safe and loved.

CHAPTER 13

THE GRADUATE-1987

A heart bursts with pride.
The same heart is breaking.
A young man in cap and gown.
Looking proud.
Justifiably so.
Looking happy.
His whole life ahead of him.
The adventure excites him.
One corner of his heart is consumed in pain.
He knows why.
He looks through the mass of faces,
Searching for just one.
His eyes meet hers-both fill with tears.
With a half-smile and a nod,
She says to him,
*"My son, I love you. I always have and
I always will. You are a man now and I must
set you free. I will miss you."*
He knows what she has said,
Through his heart, not his ears.

For eighteen years, their hearts have been bound.
He nods back to her, his pride now larger than life.
His heart answers her back.
He knows that she will hear.
"I love you, Mom. You got me this far-
stay with me for the rest of the ride.
I will thank you, but you must know that
this is not Good-bye.
This is just an intersection on the Road of
Life and I know which way I am going.
Remember, Mom, all roads lead home.
So smile, pretty lady, smile."
Quickly, he turns. His friends are waiting.
A chill goes through her -loneliness, again.
Just then, he turns toward her and makes a funny face.
She laughs in spite of herself.
She takes a deep breath.
In that one second, her pain has begun to ease.
Her little boy is alive and seemingly quite well,
And living in the heart of THE GRADUATE.

In June of 1987, a week after his high school graduation celebration, Sean and I had a confrontation. I had been on a downward spiral ever since the grad ceremonies because I had always thought that once my boys finished school they would leave me. I remember being high as a kite at the graduation banquet and I remember Sean glaring at me. I also remember falling back to earth with the speed of a comet and landing with a thud.

On the night of the week later, Sean and I had a heated

argument because I had made a nice supper for him and Janet and was looking forward to them spending the evening with me. Instead, they wanted to eat and run because there was a party they wanted to go to. I cried and begged him to not leave me, and in a moment of absolute fury, Sean said, "If I could afford it, I would move out of here. I just can't take any more of you." He and Janet then went out the door.

It would be an understatement to say that I was crushed. I did not cry. I did not scream. I calmly went into the bathroom, found my stash of pills, and got a glass of water. I put them on the table beside the phone in my bedroom. I said to myself, "I'm going to phone for help. If I find someone to help me, I'll get off the bed alive. If no one will talk to me, I'll take the pills and get this over with once and for all." Jason was in the kitchen doing the dishes and had no idea that I was as upset as I was.

I phoned my most recent therapist and he merely told me to calm down. I knew I could not phone Beth, because I knew how she felt. I phoned my mother—no answer. I phoned my brother—same thing. I phoned the Edmonton city crisis center and the line was busy. Finally, I phoned the General Hospital and asked to speak to any doctor in the emergency department. A man came to the phone, who could have been the janitor for all I knew, but he seemed to give a damn about what I was saying and that was all I needed to hear. He told me to come in right away.

I casually told Jason, who had been in the kitchen doing the dishes totally unaware of my calamity, that I was going to the hospital. When he offered to come with me, I abruptly said, "NO!" He asked me resignedly if I was really going to get there, and I said I was, but if they refused to admit me, I would make no guarantees about getting back. (Can you believe it?)

I left in the middle of the night and I am sure that Jason was beside himself with worry. But then again, I had cried wolf so often that it may have just been another day in a long sequence of ugly days.

All the way into town I focused on the task at hand—getting me into the hospital before all the horrid thoughts started taking over my mind again. When thoughts of driving off the road or into the line of a larger vehicle came into my mind, I fought them off, but I never let them get too far away in case I would have need them of them later. After what seemed an eternity, I arrived at the hospital and went straight to the emergency ward. I prayed that the person I had talked to on the phone had really been a doctor and that he was still on duty. As proof that there is a God, the man I talked to was there; bless him, he really was a doctor. Remembering my call, he took me straight into the consulting room. I must say it was the fastest that I had ever been taken care of in an emergency ward in my life.

The kind doctor listened to my story about my fight with Sean, about my bottle of pills, about my drive into town, and about my decision to stay alive long enough to talk to him. He then told me the bad news that there were no empty beds on the regular psychiatric wards, but there was one available in psychiatric lock-up. I was devastated and scared! When he saw how scared I looked, he told me that he could not let me go home after all that I had told him and he must insist that I take that one last bed. I agreed, deciding that a little time behind locked doors might not be so bad.

To my surprise, the ward was not as bad as others had led me to believe. The walls were painted warm colors and I could tell that renovations had recently been done. The nurses were really pleasant. For a moment I began to think that it was no different than the regular ward. Then the orderly who brought me left and I could hear the sound of a lock turning in the door that led out into the hallway. In a very short time, a nurse began to prep me for my stay.

First, she searched me for pills and anything that could be used as a weapon to hurt myself or anyone else. She even took the shoelaces out of my runners as they apparently have wonderful uses for the creative patient. (I guess I am not that imaginative, because it still mystifies me what I could have done with them!) My cigarettes and lighter were confiscated; I was told that I could smoke, but only in the area in front of the desk, and I had to ask a nurse to light each and every one. They were not there to teach me the dangers of smoking, so I could chain-smoke if I wanted to, but I could not have any contact with the lighter.

Next, the nurse stood and watched me change into my hospital gown and then she took all my clothes away from me. I was allowed no personal belongings that could potentially cause me harm or that could be of use if I tried to escape. I had to use the bathroom with the door open and could only use the toothpaste provided by them. The nurse showed me that the window of my room was made of Plexiglas and could not be broken. She demonstrated by banging on it with a hard object. I had to sleep with the door to my room open at all times. They did not try to keep me in my room, but even the common room was behind glass and in front of the nurses' desk for full-time viewing by those in charge.

My mother came to see me the next day and brought me my needlework. That did not go over so well when the nurses saw the needles and the scissors. Needless to say, they took them away. John came up to see me and I thought he was going to be sick right there in front of me. He had to be frisked on his way in, and then had to endure the locked doors and the restraints that were present everywhere. He could not believe his wife could be in a place like this, no matter how nicely it was decorated.

John was asked to fill out a form asking for information about me. I will always remember when he was asked how I had changed since I had been ill and he wrote in huge black letters across the page "She used to be a BLAST!" He then asked me to sign a company check that required both our signatures and was dismayed when I signed it with my maiden name. I was not trying to make any point or trying to upset him, I just momentarily forgot who I was. In two marriages, I had never made that mistake before that day. He then left and I honestly was not sure if I would ever see him again. In the coming few weeks he visited me only once. That hurt me a lot, but I figured it was better than nothing.

Later that day, a doctor with a thick European accent came to see me and told me that he was going to give me a shot to calm my anxieties. Calm me it did, but not in a way that was comforting. My body was paralyzed, but my mind, which was the part that needed to be calmed, was as active as ever. I remember feeling sheer terror that I was going to be kept like this for the duration and that they would be able to do anything they wanted to me. Now I know why the other patients talked about this place in such eerie tones. All the old movies about mental asylums came to mind and I could not move a muscle in my own defense. I do not know of any moment of fear that matched those hours on that bed under the influence of that drug. When I could finally move, I forced myself onto the floor and I crawled out to the nurses' desk and somehow got them to realize how scared I was. When they came to give me another shot, I made a "controlled" fuss and another

Marilyn Avient

doctor was called; somehow I persuaded her not let them give me another dose of that nightmarish drug. I promised to behave. She finally conceded. From then on, I had to be careful to not get too upset or they would figure that I needed calming down again.

I saw a young man in the common room one day, who was in a zombie-like state. After thinking about it for a while, I realized that he and I had been fellow patients on the psych ward in 1984. Apparently, he had tried to fly off a building thinking he was an angel. His body was mangled and to me it appeared that his soul had died but forgot to take along his body. I felt so sad seeing him like this. His name was Richard and he was a handsome young man who could not handle life because of his mental illness. I saw him like a son. He saw me like a mother. During that first stay in hospital, Richard and I had become very close and I cherished the fact that he had chosen me as his confidante. He had no visitors, so I guess he needed someone to be close to. When he left the hospital I worried about what he was going to do in the big world, and I was sad because I was really going to miss our wonderful talks and his sweet disposition.

One may question how I could say that I cared so deeply for him without keeping in touch. In most circumstances in life, this is unconscionable, but coming from a psych ward setting the way we had, it was normal and very common. I, and probably the others too, felt very misunderstood out in the real world. I was a hard person to love because I had so little love to give to even the members of my family. My inadequacies as a human being were so large and luminous that I made everyone around me feel the same way—they loved me, but I made them feel helpless and I knew that.

In hospital, I met people who were just like me and who

had no interest in trying to fix me. They were just as self-centered as I was and so we got along well. No one expected anything of anyone else, and that was really quite a relief. When I met Richard, we both felt safe with one another and we knew that no matter how close we were, it was only in the context of the walls of the hospital ward. He had nothing to do with my real life, and I had nothing to do with his. That was the way with most relationships that developed during my many weeks in psychiatric care.

Once I was home I really did not want to be reminded of my time there, so all friendships ceased as soon as I left the hospital each time. I talked on rare occasion to one or two of the women, but the conversations were strained and difficult because we had nothing in common except our illnesses. One girl told me that she had friends who could get me any pills necessary for killing myself, and so I had one of my saner moments of that time and decided she was not a person I wanted in my life. We never talked again.

I was in lock-up for three days when a bed became available on the main psychiatric ward and, coincidentally, I got the same room that I had occupied in my previous visit. There were even some patients whom I recognized from my other stays and, of course, many of the same staff members who did not seem all that thrilled to see me. I guess it gets discouraging when the same patients keep making return appearances. In spite of all this familiarity, this visit was very different. I used to be so meek and mild but because of my medications, as mentioned earlier, I was quite a different patient than the nurses had seen there before.

I was told many times to stop picking on other patients and being so mean to them. I found this to be hilarious because I had been a little mouse the last two times I was there. It also became common that in the middle of a sentence I would just go to sleep. This was really amazing because here I was surrounded by doctors and nurses, and no one paid me any mind. They had trouble waking me up, but so what? I also got heck from one nurse because she had to clean chocolate off of me in the morning. I guess after they gave me my sleeping pill, I went into my usual stupor and attacked a box of chocolate cookies; obviously, only a few of them made it to my mouth. I was covered in chocolate and so were the bed and the blankets. I was definitely not my nurse's favorite patient that day! But unbelievably no one on the medical team questioned why I did those things or why I had changed so much.

Another thing that was intensified during my depression years was my discontent with the Christian church as an institution. I was totally disillusioned by some members of the clergy and vowed I would never go to church again. Needless to say, I was not pleased when a new patient was admitted who claimed that he was Jesus of Nazareth. I felt like someone had lit a fire under me—I went ballistic and that was just on hearing about him from another patient.

When I met "Jesus" in person, it was fireworks at first sight—and I mean that in the worst possible way! He introduced himself and I told him in no uncertain terms what I thought about him *and* the guy he was claiming to be. I have never been so belligerent, so mean, so out of control around anyone in my whole life, before or since. The situation became so heated that the other patients would not stay in the same room with the two of us. What he and most of them had no way of knowing was that this was so far removed from my true personality that I, too, could have been someone else. He brought out a rage in me that felt lethal from my standpoint. The more he acted like Jesus, the more infuriated I became. I even had to be told by the head nurse that if my behavior did not change, I could be shipped out to another facility. In some respects, I loved being like that because for once I was not the one who was scared of her own shadow—I was the one who was scaring everyone else.

One night after dinner, I and several other patients were in the sitting area just looking at the city below us as it went about its business. As we were talking, my "friend from Nazareth" came into the room and the others fled like a herd of deer that heard a dog bark. We were alone. What happened next will always be a source of awe for me. That night, in this most unexpected place, I was used as a channel and, although I did not know that at the time, this incident would add strength to the foundation of spiritual beliefs that continue for me to this day.

"Jesus" stood there, feet firmly planted, waiting for the tirade to come out of my mouth as had always happened in the past. But the Universe had other plans for us that night. I opened my mouth to spew my usual spiel at him but instead . . . I could not believe the words coming out of me. The reason I know that they were not *of* me, even though they were coming *from* me, was that I was thinking other thoughts as they were being said. I was thinking such things as "What the heck is going on here?" "Who is saying those things?" "Gee, those are really nice words; I wish I could talk like that." "How cool is this? My mouth is moving and I am not doing it."

I wish that I could remember the exact words uttered through me, but probably the amount of medication running through my system at the time made that impossible; or maybe I was not supposed to remember the words because that way I could never claim them as my own, even without intending to. I do not remember what I heard, but I remember the absolute peace and stillness that I felt. I remember feeling choked up by the beauty of what I was hearing. I remember feeling love for this man, for myself, for the other patients, for the staff, for the world, and for all living beings anywhere. *Love* totally consumed me for those amazing moments.

When the words stopped, we just stood there. He had tears running down his face and so did I as he came over and kissed me on the cheek. Then he timidly said, "You aren't going to like it when I tell you who you sounded like just then." I said, "I know who I sounded like. In fact, that wasn't me talking—that was Mary, the Holy Mother." He smiled and said, "I know and thank you." Then he quietly walked away.

By the next morning, I thought we would be back to fighting again and that probably I had dreamed the whole thing, but all of us were about to get a wonderful surprise! "Jesus" walked into the dining area, said a warm hello to me, and then apologized to everyone for any wrongdoing he had done. He said that he would try to be more considerate of their feelings from then on, and that he would appreciate it if they would tell him if he said anything in the future that hurt or offended them. He promised the group that he would try to be a kinder and better person. They all sat there with their mouths gaping open. Everything he said to the other patients had been told to him by "Mary," and I was in awe of the magnitude of what I had been involved in.

He left the hospital shortly after that—left in the night, I guess. One morning, he just did not show up for breakfast. We were simply told by the nurses that he would not be back. I do not know if they really knew where he went or whether they were mystified by the fact that he had vanished. Myself, I think that he disappeared of his own volition and I even considered the possibility that he really was Jesus coming to teach some lessons to all of us. In any case, I shall never forget that man who called himself Jesus and will always be grateful to him for the opportunity he gave me to be used as a channel. No matter how many bad things I had done in the past years, I think that by being chosen to be a messenger, I was being told that, even if no one else had, God had forgiven me.

After about three weeks, I was told that my doctor wanted to meet with me in the presence of my family. We all arrived at the designated hour. Before we were half an hour into the interview, I wanted to bolt. I could see where it was all going and I was not impressed. The doctor told us that my blood tests showed that I was not clinically depressed this time like I had been on the two previous visits. He said that although I was not depressed, I was one of the saddest people he had ever met and he wanted to know why. No one had an answer, but before we left I told him that depressed people can occupy hospital beds when there is a waiting list a yard long, but sad ones cannot—I promptly checked myself out of the hospital for the last time.

CHAPTER 14

Following that stay, I felt really ashamed of myself—not to mention foolish, embarrassed, and totally hopeless. I had just gotten rid of my safety net and could hardly wrap my head around the concept of getting on with my life, because I did not have a clue how to do that. In all honesty, I have no memory now of what I did with myself for that next year. I know that I was still seeing psychologists on a regular basis, but again I am drawing blanks when it comes to actual memories. Is it possible that I actually relaxed and took it easy for a year? Perhaps . . . but I doubt it.

My search to find the right therapist was an ongoing one for me during the years immediately following that last visit. Just when I would think I had found the right one, something would happen that would tell me to move on. I would like to go into a little bit of detail about the three that affected me the most.

I started going to one therapist shortly before I went into hospital that last time. He was that male nurse who was on the psychiatric ward during my first stay, and then an instructor at the day therapy program, working towards becoming a therapist. When I found out he did counseling in the evenings, I decided to give him a try. He was a very good-looking man, and because I fell easily for any man who would sit and listen to my troubles, this was not good news. However, this did not prove to be a problem because we talked openly about the problem I had with Ivan, the psychologist in the hospital.

For the telling of this story, I shall name this therapist, Ian—in all honesty, I cannot remember what his real name was. Ian was mostly very good to me as a counselor. He worked a lot on anger problems, so I spent a fair amount of time pounding and demolishing the cushions in his office. On some visits, I could not pummel those pillows hard enough to release the pent up anger that seemed to be brewing in me all the time. Other nights we just sat and talked the way that most therapists and clients do. There are a couple of things that I remember about my time with Ian.

One night, just as I sat down, I saw a little girl in a long white dress come into the room. She did not startle me at all—in fact, I remember feeling a kind of relief just knowing she was so close to me. I felt comfortable enough with Ian to tell him of her presence; he asked me a couple of questions about her and then let the topic go. Later he said, "The little girl is sitting on the floor to the right of you, isn't she?" I said that she was and asked him how he knew. He explained that I was directing a lot of my words in that direction as though I was including someone who was sitting there in our conversation. He gave no argument; he just accepted my word that we were not alone in the room.

Later that night, as I was driving down the road going home, I turned to shoulder check over to the right. I was quite shocked this time to see the same little girl in the back seat. This time she was wearing dungarees and a tee shirt and was standing up with her chin resting on her arms that were folded on the back of the front passenger seat. In my surprise at seeing her when I was concentrating on driving, I shrieked, and consequently saw her fly out the window. I have never seen her since but Irene, my dear friend who is a psychic and a clairvoyant, has seen a little girl around me on a number of occasions. I was sad about that incident because I always felt safe—except that last time—having her around me. I told my mom about her and she said that when we moved from Dawson Creek to Edmonton in 1950, I traveled the whole way standing up in the back seat with my chin resting on my arms that were folded on top of the front passenger seat.

The other thing that Ian did for me was to teach me the follies of putting people on pedestals. One evening, I must have been talking about some male in my life with a little too much awe. Without any warning, Ian jumped up onto his desk and stood there looking down on me. Because he was over six feet tall, this made quite the scene. As he looked down at me he asked, "So how do you like talking to me like this?" I told him that I hated it and that my neck was hurting. He then said in a very firm voice, "After 40 years of doing it, your neck *should* be bloody sore! I don't know why it hasn't broken by now! So, you have two choices. You can either ask them to come down to the ground and stand beside you or you can jump up on the pedestal and put yourself at their same level. The point is that you have to make a choice and you have to make it now."

I did not know what to do, so I asked him if I could join him up there on the desk to see how it felt. He said to come on up and so we stood there for quite a while just talking as though we were sitting down. Finally, I said that this was OK, but not very practical for going about one's daily life, so I told him I wanted us to get down on the ground again. We did and I felt myself experiencing an AH-HA moment of magnanimous proportions!

A few days later when John got back from out of town, I

asked him if he would do me the favor of jumping up and standing on the pool table. To my surprise, he did, and not only that, he made it look like it was just a normal thing to do. We talked for a while with him on the table and me on the floor. I noticed my neck getting tired, so I asked him if he would be willing to come down. He said, "If I come down, you'll let me stay down, right?" I knew then that he realized where he had been all these years in relation to where I had put myself. I promised that I would not put him up on a pedestal anymore, and I believe I have kept that promise. I now admire him deeply but I do not idolize him.

To my dismay, one day Ian just disappeared. I called him but there was no answer and when I went around to his office it had been vacated. I was mystified and even a little hurt that he had not called just to tell me that he was leaving. Perhaps he could have referred me to someone else, but instead he made his leaving a big mystery. Another man creeping away in the night!

So I had to go shopping for a new therapist. One stands out in my mind because he actually made me laugh. He was soft-spoken and quiet, but when he did speak he sounded like he was in kindergarten and I was in university. I knew much more about everything including the human psyche than he did. I did not know how he even got to where he was. Then when I talked about my problems he would nod off. Once I stopped talking and he did not even notice because he was sound asleep. Needless to say one session with him was more than enough. Funny, but I always thought that I was a little more interesting than that.

My next doctor was quite the character—I shall call him Dr. White. I had heard him on a radio show and was quite pleased when I was able to get in to see him. He was unique in that he was the only psychiatrist I ever had who told me some of his own personal little quirks. For instance, he was a choco-holic and he had not spoken to his parents in 15 years. There were other intimate details of his life that I really did not need to know. I did not like him "sharing" because I figured that it was my hour and we should only be talking about me. He was funny and maddening; those are not always traits that one looks for in a therapist. However, I plodded on, because he was so different from any professional that I had ever gone to for help.

One day I left the office after having an extensive discussion about suicide. As I was walking out the door, I turned around and said, "Of course I'm afraid to die but I'm even more afraid to live." Next afternoon, I turned on his radio show and was dismayed to hear that his topic for the day was "Afraid to die! Afraid to live!" It was so strange to sit in my home and listen to *my* story on the radio. He made an error and I actually had the guts to phone in and tell him on the air that if he was going to use my story then he had better get it right. The next week, when I was leaving his office after our session, I asked him what material he would like for his show this week. I then told him that I did not appreciate what he had done. I think that was the most assertive I had ever been in my life!

I think Dr. White's aim was to make me feel crazier than I already felt myself to be. At every appointment he said, at least once, that we had to sue Ivan, the therapist, for his bad behav-ior. I agreed that he had been very unprofessional, but I told him over and over again that I would not drag myself or my family through a lawsuit. I just felt too guilty about my part in it. I knew the facts, but I did not quite accept them. Nonetheless, I got very tired of hearing about it.

On another day, in 1988, I was telling him about Andrew,

my stepson, who died a premature death in 1994 from drug abuse. I had been very afraid of Andrew because people who use drugs say and do some very scary things. Usually Dr. White wrote down a lot of notes during a visit, but this time he stopped and even got very dramatic by putting his notepad into his drawer. I asked him why, and he said, "I do not want to be tempted to write any of this down because I want to protect you. You see, I think you are going to kill Andrew one day. When the police come to my office, I will not be lying when I tell them that I have no record of any discussion about him." Very strange man, indeed! I always thought that the wrong one of us was sitting with the jar of chocolates behind the desk.

And on yet another day . . . after telling him about my rages while on the antidepressant called Nadir, he laughed and gave me a prescription for it because he said he thought it would be interesting to see me get that angry. I did not fill the prescription. I continued seeing Dr. White until the day he told me to "go home and divorce John and put us all out of our misery."

Sometime in 1988, I heard about ACOA, or Adult Children of Alcoholics, and was allowed into the group because, even though there were no alcoholics in my immediate family, there had been some in my recent ancestry. My father never allowed himself to touch a drop of alcohol, so there had never been any drinking in our house—*ever*. At first I felt out of place because once again I seemed to be the only one who did not have any obvious addiction or abuse problems in her background. However, what was interesting was that this was the first place where I had to be "well" to be there— no mood-altering prescriptions were allowed. That, in itself, was a big turning point for me. I also realized that although I did not have the obvious problems in my family like most of the others, I felt exactly the same way that they felt. For once I felt like I fit in somewhere.

As time went on and as we studied family dynamics, I realized that my family operated much the same way that an alcoholic family did. My father was what is called "a dry drunk" because he was *so* adamant about *not* drinking. Apparently, that is almost as problematic as being an alcoholic. Interestingly enough, my mother had many of the traits of being an enabler and each of us kids fit one of the roles that children of alcoholics take on.

I learned a lot about myself in that group and it was the first time that a group of regular people saw me as a very honest, courageous person. They saw the crazy-making patterns of my childhood and so I began to see them too. All of a sudden some things made sense and I was relieved. Alcoholic families who do not address the problem are said to have an elephant in the middle of the living room that everyone just ignores. It is not until someone asks "Has anyone noticed that there is a flippin' elephant in the living room?" that anything can change. When I heard about that elephant, I understood it because I had seen and felt it in our house for all of my life, especially when my dad was in a sad mood. All of a sudden I felt a little less crazy.

CHAPTER 15

My father and I had a relationship that made my heart purr. I have two theories about why we were so close: The first is that I believe very strongly that he and I have shared many lifetimes together and so, on a soul level, we are very close. The second and more mundane reason is that he was the one who was there with me when I almost died of pneumonia when I was 2 years old. No matter what, I seemed to be the child who could make him smile regardless of what mood he was in. I truly believe that my father had his own depression to deal with. Perhaps it was just regret about things he had not done with his life; nonetheless, he looked sad a lot of the time—thus the elephant in the room. It was my self-appointed duty to keep Dad smiling; that is where Lulubelle came in. The sad "me" could not make him smile, but she could.

In the year that I was attending sessions of ACOA, Mom and I talked a lot about our life with Dad. I told her how difficult it was to be in charge of keeping Dad happy. She told me that she had no idea that I had felt so obliged to do that for all those years, but then she surprisingly added, "Thank you, Judy, for taking on that task and doing it so well. I'm sorry it has been so hard on you, but I want you to know that I was always so grateful when you got your dad to laugh. You know what you did? You kept the bomb from exploding." I was stunned into silence—I had no idea that anyone else knew about the bomb. Now, when I talk about a bomb—I do not think we were not expecting a physical blowup because Dad was a very gentle man but, in all honesty, I really am not sure just what form it *would* take. The interesting thing is that Mom and I had both used the word *bomb* in our heads without ever having discussed it before. So, perhaps, between her love and dedication and my entertaining skills, a tragedy of some kind was averted. That day, Mom made my efforts seem not only worthwhile, but important as well.

I have a number of memories about my dad when I was child, but these are my two favorites. Dad was in the army for all my years growing up. My biggest thrill was watching him march on the parade grounds on Saturday mornings. The military band would be playing wonderful marching music. While his platoon marched by the stands, I would wait with baited breath to see if he would do it—I was rarely disappointed: he would turn his head as much as he could and, as he marched by, he would wink at me. That was a happy moment. To this day, I cannot hear a marching band play without crying in happy remembrance.

The other one happened every Christmas morning. At 6:00 am, it was a tradition that Dad and I would go out into the snowy darkness and drive to pick up his sister, my aunt. It was usually very cold, and the windows were never completely fog free, but we had such good talks on those rides that we never minded. There were very few cars on the road at that hour, and tree lights were twinkling in the houses along the way so to me it felt like a mystical winter wonderland. The ride home was not as memorable but it was quite enjoyable because my aunt was one of my favorite people when I was a child; she was funny, she always told good stories, and she gave wonderful store-bought gifts.

I was also very proud of my dad because he was a lay-minister in the United Church. His dream had been to be a full-fledged minister, but he dropped out of school in grade 7. No one would ever know this because he was articulate when he spoke, he was a good writer, he gave wonderful sermons, and he could talk intelligently about world events. I loved it when he took over a Sunday service because his sermons were full of stories; this made them much more interesting than those of the regular clergy.

In 1969, Dad was diagnosed with emphysema, the result of many years of heavy smoking. This is a very bad way to die as it is, basically, slow suffocation. When you cannot breathe, it is tough to do many of the things you want to do. He did a lot of writing then because he could just sit in his armchair and relax; it was something for which he did not need any extra breath. He and I still got along wonderfully, but as an adult, we tended to argue a little. However, when I reverted to being the doting child, we got along just fine. When we knew his time was running short, my brother, David, and I went to say good-bye. Dad said good-bye to my brother, but instead of saying the same to me, he told me that he would write soon. He died in the wee hours of the morning on April 14, 1977, and so once again he snuck away in the night without saying good-bye to me. I took a long while to get over that.

I remember being angry at my dad after he died, but now I am not sure why. Of course, there is the obvious reason that I was angry because he had left me, but I do not think that was all of it. I remember wishing that he would have let me grow up instead of wanting me to remain his little girl forever. If he had, perhaps I would have grown up a little faster. I remember wishing that he would encourage me to do the things that scared me. If he had, maybe I would have been motivated by my fear instead of being paralyzed by it. I remember wishing that he would tell me that I could do anything I set my mind to. If he had, I might have been more ambitious and more willing to take risks. Most of all, I wished he would have told me that it was not my responsibility to make him happy. If he had, perhaps I would have told my son the same thing much sooner. He never did any of those things, but much, much later I realized he could not teach what he did not know, so I had to forgive him. I worked very hard to unearth all of the things about Dad that kept me in the grips of anger—I unearthed them, dealt with them, and now I have let them go. I am now at peace with my dad.

Please note that the paragraph below is only about those patients who truly did not have suppressed memories. However, after being given the suggestion of them over and over again, they began to think that they did, indeed, have them; in reality, they did not.

In the 1980s it was very trendy to discover repressed memories that were usually about abuse or something equally unpleasant. The doctor would tell the patient that the fear of the pain of remembering was the reason why he or she had tucked them away where they would not be found again. When the patient could not come up with his or her own bona fide horrific memories, some doctors were not above suggesting things repeatedly until that patient came to believe some long-forgotten memory really had surfaced. The doctors tried very hard to do that to me.

Many medical personnel told me that my dad and I were *too* close, so there must have been some abuse. I would say there was not and they would argue that there was. In the medicated, vulnerable, doctor-worshiping state that I was in, I began to question myself and wondered if they could possibly know

Marilyn Avient

something that I did not. At one point, I was convinced they, being doctors, must be right so I told my family that it had happened. No one believed me and I know that I hurt my mother very badly. Once I stopped seeing those doctors, I began to realize that nothing bad had ever happened. However, no matter how hurt Mom may have been, she did something for me that I will never forget.

Sometime after my last hospital stay, Mom called me and said she had to see me soon. We made a date for the following night. I was nervous because Mom had sounded very strange on the phone. When she arrived, she had a newspaper in her hand; she was ashen white and very nervous. She told me that we had better get this over with because she felt like she could vomit at any moment. I became very scared about what I was going to hear from her. Then without any warning she said, "Did your father ever molest you or touch you inappropriately?" After I picked myself up, I told her that I had no memory of it and that I doubted it very much.

That may sound like a wishy-washy answer but, as I said, when I was in the hospital doctors were always trying to make my relationship with my dad look not only bad, but quite dastardly. They insisted we were too close for a father and daughter. However, just having Mom ask me that question made me feel very certain that nothing untoward had ever happened.

Mom then opened the newspaper. It was a full-page write-up of a girl who had been molested by her father; basically, her story sounded just like mine, except that she was sure of the abuse. Our pain seemed to be eerily similar. I could not explain that part, except to say that "pain is pain" not matter what caused it, but I knew, all of a sudden, that my beloved father had never, ever touched me in an improper way. Mom began to cry and she said that when she read it, she thought she was seeing the story of my breakdown right in front of her eyes. She said, "I have to know it isn't true, because the last words I heard from your father were 'I love you, Florencie.' He called them out with the last little bit of air that remained in his lungs as I walked out of his room on that last night of his life. I have to know if I can trust those last words of his, and only you can tell me that." (Dad always called Mom "Florencie," rather than "Florence," which sounded too formal.)

I assured her that nothing had ever happened, and I held her as she cried. Then she held me as I cried. I made myself a promise that night that I have tried very hard to keep, but it would take a number of years before I actually fulfilled it. I promised myself and God that I would never doubt my mother's love again. This was one of only a handful of times when I knew beyond a shadow of a doubt that my mom *did* love me. It was plain to see that she would have believed me no matter what I had said. At that moment, I felt a glimmer of hope that there really was love and life out there—and it was shown to me by my mother.

CHAPTER 16

Suicide! Suicide! Suicide! I am sick of writing about it and I am sure you are sick of reading about it. I never really wanted to kill myself, but I wanted everyone to think that I did. In hospital I did some things (such as giving belongings away) that were on the checklist for potential suicide, but little did they know because I was just trying to get people to like me and to think that I was special. Because I fit the pattern, the hospital personnel labeled me as "suicidal."

When Sean told me, in 1987, he wished he could get away from me, I did want to *die* because I could not imagine living without him, but I did not want to *kill* myself. I was just ashamed, sad, and scared that my main lifeline was going to desert me. But I had to be considered suicidal to be believed that I needed help. I was not lying, because it was all done subconsciously, and only upon looking back am I beginning to understand it. There really should be more words to describe *lacking the life force* other than *wanting to off oneself.*

For the first 35 years of my life I thought that my family could and would not be able to survive without me. I saw myself as the glue that held everyone together, and although that was a pressure in itself, I believed it with all my heart and soul. It is no wonder that my lifelong melancholy turned to deep-seated depression in the years after my dad's death, because that was the first indication that my family *was* falling apart.

When I broke down in my 36th year, all of that changed. I did not want to be needed for anything anymore. I wanted someone else to take care of all the silly details of life and I definitely gave up the role of family caretaker. In fact, when I was in hospital the first time, I was jealous when I would hear that one of the patients had succeeded in committing suicide when he or she was out on a pass. That person was out of the rat race and felt the pain no more. I was envious when I would hear that someone had died of natural causes. That person went in a respectable manner. In reality, I was tired, tired, tired. All I wanted was rest.

So if I had no reason to live, the only alternative was to want to die. There are no words in the English language to adequately describe the absence of life in a body without it being dead. In fact, that *is* the definition of *death* if I am not mistaken. Then there is *lifeless*, which again means dead or dying. What about *life-lacking*? Perhaps I could coin a new phrase with that one. But this was my subconscious dilemma: How do I say that I have no reason or inclination to live without declaring a wish to die?

I began to obsess about dying and how to do it. The more I thought about it, the more I wanted to think about it. The payoffs for staying in this frame of mind were limitless:

Nothing was expected of me.

The patients at the hospital accepted me.

My family began to believe that I was really sick and that saved me hiding from them.

I knew that I really did have an "out" if my situation got bad enough.

I did not have to look for a job.

I did not even have to try to make a life for myself.

The hospital staff believed it, so my family did too.

I got more attention at the hospital.

If I did give up and do something to harm myself, no one would be surprised.

With all of these reasons to stay in that blackness, why would I consider leaving? I really began to believe that I was suicidal, so I planned concrete ways to prove it. From 1984 to 1987 I extracted a few pills out of every prescription and made myself a "safety stash." During my months out of hospital, I would sit on the bathroom floor almost every day, line them up according to color, and then count them over and over again. The highest count was 200. These pills that I saved to kill myself one day, actually became my lifesavers because, even without using them, they were my hope that the pain in my mind did not have to be forever. If I needed them, they were there. In 1987, after my stay in hospital, Sean and John stood over me until I flushed every one of those pills down the toilet. I tried to tuck some away, but my guards were eagle-eyed and caught me every time.

I found out later that Sean and Jason made the walk from the school bus very slowly every day during those years. They were both sure that one day they would come in the house and find me dead. After all, mothers never lie and I had told them that it would happen one day. I shall never forgive myself for instilling such fear into my young sons' hearts. Many times when they came home from school, I would be asleep on my bed. They told me later that they always came in to make sure that I was breathing. I am so sorry for causing that pain.

When the pills were gone I began to plan goofy things like going out onto the highway that was close to our house all dressed in black and waiting for a big truck to come by that could hit me. I wrote letters to everyone to say my last words to them. When I found them in later years, I was glad they never received them because the letters were not that nice. Another time I told Sean that he would have to make sure no one was angry after I did the dastardly deed because I would not be able to handle them all hating me. In actuality, they probably had pretty bad feelings about me just because I was so obsessed with dying. I also bet they sometimes wished I would just do it and get it over with. Imagine how different my life would have been in those years if I had been equally obsessed with *living*.

I knew that deep down inside I just wanted attention and, even though my pain was real, I just wanted someone to figure that out. I am sure about this because one night when I was feeling very low, I called the Crisis Center and a young man kept me on the phone for hours. After a couple of hours I became mighty sick of his voice, but somehow he kept me on the line until the acute urges to harm myself had passed. When morning arrived and I was still alive, I went into yet another form of despair because I had been too cowardly to actually do it. This nice young man told me to think of it as a victory—I had made it through a very tough night. For some reason that felt good and I tried to give myself credit for being courageous enough to live through the intense pain.

After that night, I received a weekly call from a woman at the Distress Line and this went on for about three months. With all the people in my life who loved me, it now seems odd that the caring voice of a stranger should mean so much to me. Sometimes we would talk for an hour, and sometimes we only talked for a few minutes, depending on what my state of mind was that day. John was very impressed with this charitable organization who took the time to call me each week, but I also think he was sad that I could talk to them but I would not talk to him about these very personal matters. The reason for this was simple. He was too close to the situation and I knew that I could not talk to him about my obsession about death and dying. He would take it personally and the stranger was able to look at it with more objectivity. Because I was sure John was going to leave someday anyway, I did not want to give him another reason to make that departure come any sooner.

I did not know how I was ever going to get out of this state of mind, but lo and behold help was in sight and it came from an unlikely, yet totally sensible source—my dad. In 1989 I had visions on two separate evenings that cleared up this problem for good. On both occasions, I was in bed and I was in that place that one slips into just before falling sleep. On the first night, I saw my father in the middle of large group of people. He stood out from the rest, and even from a distance I could see he was wearing a maroon-colored shirt that I instinctively knew was made of soft and cozy flannel.

Dad turned and saw me watching him, and beckoned to me with his hand. For some reason, unbeknown to me, I merely turned away and forced myself back into a state of full awareness. I did not feel like I had had a dream; I felt like I had just seen my Dad and had ignored his overtures to me. I could hardly believe I had dismissed him like that.

A few nights later, the second dream occurred, again just before I fell into a deep sleep. This time Dad saw me sooner than he had the first time. He was wearing the same maroon shirt, and once more I reacted to the wonderful texture, even though I had never touched it. This time, the crowd went quiet, and opened up to allow him to walk toward me. Again, he motioned to me to follow him, but this time, he said, "Come, my Judy, follow me!" My heart leapt at the sound of his voice. He was smiling that smile that used to tell me that everything was OK in my world. I melted. I stood there for what seemed like a long time, but was probably only a few seconds. Then I slowly shook my head, and he smiled even more. He stood there for a moment watching me, then he waved and turned away. The crowd closed in around him and he was gone. I woke myself up. I was crying.

Given the chance, I never thought that I would turn down an invitation to go be with Dad. I had been thinking about killing myself, for months by that time, and lo and behold, I turned down an offer to die. I turned down an offer to be with my father forevermore. If I had walked toward him, I know that I would have just died in my sleep—so easy, so painless. But I did not do it! I actually went into a depressed slump for a few days. Thoughts of suicide were no longer of any comfort. I had had my chance, and I let it slip away.

Only years later did I realize that my Dad had given me an ultimatum. He obviously knew about my thoughts of death, so, in essence, he said to me, "Die . . . or live. You have to choose. Right now you exist in a living death, which is wasting the gift of life that you got from God through your mother and I. Come with me, or get on with it." With the help of a dream, I chose to live. On some level, which was out of my cognitive range, I knew that I had a lot more living to do. I was scared to live, because I had no idea how to do that, but I knew that I would have to try. After that night, I never thought about killing myself again. For the second time, my Dad gave me life.

I do not think this lesson could have come from anyone other than Dad. I trusted him with my soul and perhaps that was part of our contract with one another. Although I stopped thinking about dying on an hourly basis, it took me a while to get the knack of living. I am so glad that I did not choose to die because I now have so many wonderful reasons to live; the most important one is that I have gotten to know and like myself. I can even say with confidence that I love myself. *Until I can live for myself, I cannot live for anyone else.*

I asked my mom the next day if Dad had ever owned a maroon shirt. She said, "Yes, but you wouldn't have seen it. I know that because I remember when you and John left our place on your last visit, I went out shopping and spotted this shirt. Your dad had been so cold and this shirt looked so warm and cozy. He loved that shirt and he wore it every single day until he went to hospital (where he died). He always said that it was his favorite shirt, ever. I had to wash it at night because he wouldn't go even one day without wearing it. Why do you ask?" I told her about the dreams. She was awestruck, and so was I. I have often said that I am never *surprised* when I realized that God has stepped into my life to help me, but I am always *amazed.*

THE VISITATION

I saw my Dad amidst a crowd,
He turned and he saw me.
He beckoned me to follow him-
I pretended not to see.

The crowd, it had no faces
As though all alone he stood.

Forced myself back to consciousness,
My heart, it felt like wood.

Not many nights passed by me
'Til the same crowd passed my view.
Again, same face I recognized,
He looked up as though on cue.

This time he stepped out of the crowd,
He motioned me with his hand,
"Come, my Judy, follow me!"
I turned away at his command.

I awoke and I was crying,
Non-belief at what I had done.
Given the chance, I thought I would follow him
Like the moon daily follows the sun.

That dream, it was a message,
Only now I see it so clear.
For years, I have felt so guilty,
But I could not shed a tear.

What my Dad was offering me
Is not easy to explain.
If I had agreed to follow him,
Today I would feel no pain.

He let me know that I had a choice
To die or else to live.
If such an offer could be refused,
There must be more that I have to give.

CHAPTER 17

In 1988, two life-changing events happened for our family. The first was that after being on the market for two years, our house at South Cooking Lake finally sold. To our chagrin, it was bought for much less than it was worth, but we had to take what we could so we could finally get me out of that house. Being isolated out in the country had not been good for me. We moved back into Edmonton where we had to settle for renting a condo because we did not have enough money to buy another house.

The other event was that Sean and Janet, both only 19 years of age, got engaged, scheduling their wedding for August 12, 1989. I was not prepared emotionally for the loss of my son in one of life's milestones (again!), so I panicked at the prospect of dealing with the wedding, in particular, and the marriage, in general. This was not new, because I went into a tailspin at all my sons' major life events—most notably: taking their first steps, starting kindergarten, getting their driver's licenses, starting to shave, going on a date, graduations, and moving away from home. You name it—if my boys did anything for the first time, I flipped out! But, my God, a wedding—this seemed to be the real deal. The despair I felt was more than overwhelming. The day of the wedding kept looming closer, but I was not getting any nearer to feeling like I could handle it. However, I need not have worried because the Universe was making plans for me; I just did not know it. In May, three months before the wedding, I was given the name of a psychotherapist who was a little different than most others in his field. The only catch was that this man was so popular that he had a six-month waiting list. I shall call him Dr. Radner. I phoned his office as soon as I heard about him and got my name on the list. I was told that it could possibly be about six months before there would be an opening.

The next day I had a particularly bad day and could not seem to get out of the pit I had jumped into immediately upon rising that morning. I went outside thinking that some sunshine might help. As I walked, I prayed to God, saying, "Please, dear God, send me some help. Please. I don't know what to do next." Not feeling any better, I went home. As I unlocked the door to our condo, I heard the phone ringing. It was Dr. Radner's receptionist asking me if I would like to have an appointment the next day because there had been a cancellation. Of course, I said that I would and I spent the rest of the day in a much better state of mind, knowing that my pleas for help had been answered.

When I got to his office the next day, I told the receptionist what had happened. She said that she hears those stories all the time. Then she leaned forward and said, "Would you believe that I called 30 people before I called you—either they didn't answer or they couldn't come in today. Obviously you were the one who was meant to be here today." And so began one of the greatest adventures of my life.

I was not all that impressed with Dr. Radner on my first visit. He did not smile much, speak much, or ever refer to me by name. I really wondered what the fuss was all about. However, he did say that he would see me for five visits only and then we would reassess if more would be required. I briefly told him my life's story and came back the second time expecting more of the same.

On the second visit, he was just as aloof, and he still would not call me by my name. After this went on for a number of sessions, I asked him why he refused to acknowledge me. He replied, "Why is that so important to you? Will my stating your name make you feel more visible? I want you to think about that." In that second session, he asked me questions that were different from what I had ever been asked before. Then he asked me a question that I cannot remember, which surprises me because its repercussions were huge. Perhaps I am not meant to remember it; I can accept that. Anyway, he asked me this question and I answered it truthfully from my heart. Upon hearing my answer, he gave this wonderful smile and said, "And now we can begin."

I asked him what was happening because all of a sudden the energy in the room had changed. Dr. Radner explained that he uses that question with some people as a test. There is no right or wrong answer, but the answer tells him whether this person is operating from the mind, or from the heart and soul. My answer told him that my sadness was not in my head and I was not mentally ill; rather, my soul was permeated with grief and sorrow. This was where we were going to work. I felt like he had really heard me. I told him that I had always felt like the only English-speaking person in a room full of foreign-speaking people. They could not understand me and I could not understand them. *Finally* another English-speaking person had entered the room. That was one of the most exciting days of my life. Glory be, now I knew I was going to get well!

For the next couple of months we worked very hard. My aim was twofold. First of all, I wanted to understand *why* it was so hard for me to let go of Sean. Secondly, I wanted to know *how* I was going to do it. By the time August 12 rolled around, I had made major changes; Dr. Radner said that he had never seen a client work any harder than I had done. I asked him and his wife to come to the church to attend the wedding ceremony because only he knew what I had gone through to prepare for this event. They came and I felt safer just knowing he was there—yes, it was *that* big of a deal for me.

A couple of things happened that I would like to relate. I was feeling quite slighted because Janet's parents were part of the ceremony and they had the opportunity to actually say publicly that they were giving her away to Sean in marriage. I know that it is merely a ritual that is slightly out of date now, but it still makes them feel like they have some say in the whole thing. The groom's parents are not included in the ceremony, and I decided to do something about that.

A week before the wedding, Janet asked me to go with her for the final fitting of her gown because her mom lived down East, so she was not able to be there with her. I felt honored to be asked, and afterwards we went for coffee. I told her that on every level I felt like Sean was being taken from me, which was more than I could handle. I asked her if she would be willing to take part in our own private ritual, so at least I would feel better inside. She agreed. This is what we did.

First, Sean escorted his father Dan and his stepmother to the front pew where the four of us were to sit. He did the same for us, with John and me walking on either side of him. I had specifically requested that Sean take us down the aisle just before he went to stand in front of the altar to wait for Janet. John entered the pew first and sat down. I then reached up and hugged Sean. I whispered to him that I wanted him to go to Janet and I would let him go with love. I had explained to him earlier that I was the first person to hold him when he came into the world and I wanted to be the last to hold him as he entered the next and longest phase of his life. He told me he loved me and then went to the front of the church to wait for his bride.

Janet then came down the aisle on her father's arm and, as planned, she looked me in the eye as though she had a question to ask me. With all the excitement I was touched that she remembered and took the time to do this for me. In that split second I looked deep into her eyes, and nodded my consent. She thanked me with an almost imperceptible nod of her own, and walked on to stand with Sean. In the space of about three seconds, I was made to feel like I had had my say. I felt empty, but whole and fulfilled, all at the same time. Other than Janet, only Dr. Radner knew that any of this had happened because I had told him of my plan. I am so grateful to Sean and Janet for granting me my wish.

Dr. Radner and his wife slipped away after the ceremony without a word. He knew what his presence had meant to me. He knew that he had just seen our months of work come together in a way that was very special. He knew that what he had seen me do, seemingly effortlessly, had actually wrenched my heart out by its roots. Only *he* knew, from our time together, the magnitude of that wrenching.

I had one more chance to prove that I was truly letting Sean go, and I actually did not do very well at it. However, Sean saved the day. Towards the end of the dance at the reception, and just before the bride and groom were to leave, I went outside to stand on the balcony all by myself. It had been an exhausting and unbearably hot day and I wanted some fresh air. Before long, Sean came out and joined me. He put his arm around my shoulder. We just stood there knowing that an ending had happened for us that day. (I was not ready just yet to acknowledge the *beginning* that was also there.) Tears started streaming down my face; he knew that I wanted him to take care of me as he had always done. Instead, he took my arm and tucked it into his and said, "Come with me, Mom. I've got just what you need." I thought I had won. I thought that he would take on his role as my caretaker again, but he had other things in mind. He took me over to John, and unhooked my arm out of his, and wrapped it into John's arm saying, "Mom, *this* is the man who is going to take care of you from now on."

I admit to being stunned—for two reasons. One, Sean really was stepping out of his role as caretaker. Two, I was shocked that I had not seen my husband in that role before. Because John was away working all the time I had just never let him get that close to me. As you know, I always thought that if he saw me as the needy woman that I was, he would be gone. As you will also remember, I saved all my neediness for my sons and put on a show for John. Healthy living was getting closer, but at the moment it was still a long way off.

CHAPTER 18

When I was in high school, I determined that I was not smart enough to go to university like so many of my friends had done. I saw myself as having the brains of a gnat, so I belittled myself in my own mind and said that I needed something easier. I went to a technical school to become a lab tech; to my surprise, it turned out to be a much more difficult course than I thought. I studied hard and, consequently, I did very well at it, but I still would not give myself any credit for being a good student. I told myself that I was mistaken and that it must be a very easy course if *I* could get good grades in it. That was really crazy thinking because I had always gotten good marks in school, but I diminished this by reminding everyone about how hard I had to study. As though that is a sign of weakness and a lack of intelligence! Of course this took place in 1967–1968, which was long before my breakdown, so I was still in the self-destruct mode that was very difficult to maintain with any degree of happiness.

In 1989, after Sean got married, I decided to go to university to get that monkey off my back. Jason was a freshman and Sean was in his third year; it was fun for me to have something in common with my boys. However, they did much better than me on the persistence scale; I only lasted one year, but what a year it was! Because of my need to study everything to death,

I only took three courses and, if I remember correctly, I dropped one of them. I found that 24 hours a day was not long enough for me to study to score the 9's (on a scale of 3–9) that I insisted on getting in each of my courses. I was the oldest student in my English class and the professor let me use my life, rather than the library, for my research. He loved my papers and through him I was invited to transfer to the Honors English program the following year. I was truly honored, but knew that I could not handle that kind of course load. Somehow, after all my therapy, I still found a way to make the implications of that recommendation benign and meaningless. I still lived a life of sabotaging every potentially happy or rewarding scenario in my life.

I found a psychologist at the university who guided me on a whole other route through the maze of my mind. His name was Adam, and this very good man gave me many gifts; he said I did the same for him. The first thing Adam told me was that he would not see me a second time until I made a list of 25 good things about my father. I told him I could not, and would not, do that. He told me that if that was the way I felt, then he refused to see me again. He explained to me that he does not tolerate "parent bashing" in his practice. I went home, quite irate at the audacity of the man, but sat down anyway to see if I could think of anything good about my dad. As you can see my love/hate relationship with my dead father was still in full force. I had no idea that Adam, a virtual stranger to me, was about to change all that. I could not believe it; instead of 25 things, I astonished myself by making a list of 35 things I loved and admired about my dad. *My healing and coming to peace with my dad began with that list.* What I really loved was that I saw so many of my father's talents in myself; amazingly, I had never acknowledged them before.

Adam helped me to see how cleansing it is to laugh at one-self—in other words to "not take life so seriously." Between him and Dr. Radner, I felt like I had the best of all worlds as far as emotional and spiritual support were concerned. When it came time for me to leave Adam's care, I thanked him for all that he had done for me and he said, "If you have to thank me, then I must thank you, because *when two people dance together it is never just for the benefit of one of the partners.*" I never forgot that and I was grateful for the credit he gave to me so willingly.

FINALLY TO MY DAD

The anger is behind me.
The words have all been said.
I wish that you could hold me,
But no . . . you still are dead.

I loved you, then I hated you
With all my heart and soul.
You went away, I waited . . .
Many years, I was not whole.

Now I am well; I see you smile.
Time now to say, "Forgive."
On pleasant thoughts I'll spend a while,
In peace, I yearn to live.

You and Mom, to me gave life,
I know you did your best.
The anger and the pain are gone,
I love you . . . now you rest.

1948 Me, Dad, Mom,
Barbara, Sharon

A happy picture of me 1950

Me and Paddy, my coal field friend 1950

Marilyn Avient

1953 My sisters, me & baby David. Dad is in Holland

Aren't we adorable?
Dave and me 1957

The four siblings 1956

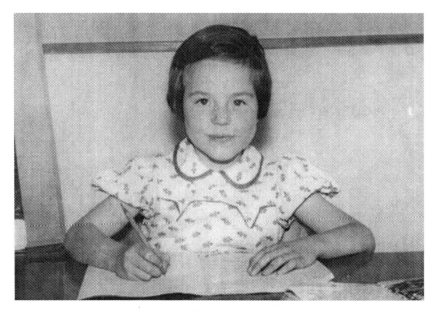

1956 Aren't I serious?

Mom circa 1957

My favorite picture
of my dad.

Marilyn Avient

1968 Medical Lab Tech
graduation picture

Dan, Sean, and me 1969

My favorite picture of my boys!

Sean and Jason 1973
Angels!

We are marrying John today!
March 19, 1977

Me, Pat (my sis-in-law), Dave
(brother) and Mom painting house
at S.Cooking Lake 1978

John and me 1981 in our
matching sweaters!

Sean, Lindsey, Andrew,
and Jason 1980

Very serious Sean, 1985
(16 yrs old)

Marilyn Avient

Sean Grade 12
Grad 1987

Jason Grade 12
Grad 1988

Starting on the
road to health
1988

Sean and me on
morning of his
wedding 1989

Sean and Janet
Aug 12, 1989

John and me at
25th Anniversary
party March 2002

My mom and Ceili 2002

Lindsey and me
Vancouver Island
Dec 2003

Last picture with Mom Sept 2004

Marilyn Avient

Jason and Sean 2004

Sean and me 2005

Happy days! John and me 2005

Sibling reunion 2006 Barb, Sharon, me, David

OUT OF . . . .

So tired of waiting for rescue,
I started relieving each shelf
Of the cobwebs, dust, and garbage
That I had gathered and heaped on myself.
The cobwebs were sticky and wanted to stay,
The dust was thick and black.
The garbage was heavy and painful to move-
No matter I made my attack.
I cleaned until I thought I would drop.
Some told me to let the dust lie . . .
I knew that I must keep working
Or I would choke on the dust and die.

Excerpt from
"Happiness Where Are You?"
The Girl Behind the Closed Door
by Marilyn Avient

CHAPTER 19

I have attended many workshops and seminars during my life, but only one of them had a life-changing impact for me. It was one of the scariest things I have ever put myself through, but also one of the most profound. There was a lot of "in your face" content, but eventually the honesty of it gave it value. I spent much of 1999 attending these workshops and, later on, being a member of the team on two different occasions. I was forced to look at some aspects of myself from which I had previously shrunk away, and as much as I hated the process, I loved it at the same time. Facing my fear, head on, set me free.

In this series of seminars, I did some of the things that totally violated my childhood survival rules. Where I formerly had vowed to never have any male friends, I found a good friend in a man named Howie who has enriched my life in many ways. I am so grateful that he helped me to overcome this fear and to throw away a rule that never should have followed me into adulthood.

Where I had formerly vowed to never make a spectacle of myself for fear people would laugh at me or to be dirty for fear that I would be punished with humiliation, one event at this seminar changed all that—even if just for that one day. With the task of impersonating my alter ego, I arrived in grubby clothes, with dirt rubbed over my face, my hair all greasy and sticking out every which way, and most difficult of all, *without my dentures!* Up until then not even my husband had seen me without my teeth. Because I always attempted to be seen with makeup perfectly applied and every hair in place, this was definitely my opposite persona. My fellow participants knew the courage it took to come out in front of them with no teeth. Who would think that such a simple act could bring such personal victory? That was but one of many because I really laid myself on the line for all three seminars. From that time on, I began to clue into the fact that I really had the potential to be a winner—in life!

The depth of these seminars helped me to hone the rough edges of the beautifully regal and deeply spiritual purple amethyst that, I realized, *is* me. I had never been quite able to see the value of *me*, but during those days in that intense setting, I came to see myself as I had never done before. This inner illumination was shown to me in no uncertain terms during one of my stints as a team member.

I was sitting alone at the team's table at the back of the room on the second to last day of the seminar. One of the windows along the top of the back wall was open just a crack as always. It was a cloudy day outside, but suddenly the sun broke forth and one beam shined through the open window directly onto me. The facilitator looked over and gasped; I was completely lit up—no other part of the room or anyone else in it was affected at all. She had done countless seminars in that hall and she told me that she had never seen anything like it before. I could feel the light bathing me and I knew something special was happening. As strange as it seems, I felt blessed and chosen. The next day, the exact same thing happened and once more the facilitator saw it. She came over to me and said, "Something really special is coming for you—you looked absolutely holy in that light." I could not argue with her because that was how I felt. Sometimes a feeling defies description, but on that day I knew that a new and brighter path lay ahead of me.

One of the direct effects of these courses came to me one day when we were staying out at our lake lot at Pigeon Lake, Alberta. Without any prethought, I told John that I had to return home for a day or so because I had something important to do. He knew that I was prone to impulsive actions so he just kissed me good-bye and wished me luck in whatever it was that I had to do. What a great guy, huh?

I headed for home with the surety of a person on a life or death mission—to me, that is exactly what I was doing. I got home, went straight to my office, and started to write an apology to my sons in long hand. I had tried apologizing to them in the past, but they always excused me, saying things such as "It's OK, Mom, you were sick" or "We were kids in the seventies; all parents did strange things then." There were also times during my earlier apologies that I tried to explain my actions, as so many people do when they think they are apologizing. So often you hear people give an apology such as "I'm sorry I hurt your feelings . . . BUT [I was having a bad day]" and they think that has done the trick. They would be wrong; *as soon as the word BUT comes into an apology, it is not an apology—it is a justification.*

On the first page of my apology I unequivocally said that I was so very sorry for everything that I had done wrong to them when they were growing up. I told them that they did not deserve any of my actions and it did not matter that I was "sick" or "crazy" or "overmedicated." I was just plain sorry. Then I listed each thing I was apologizing for without any explanation or embellishment. I asked them not to show this document to anyone else because I did not need the judgment that would ultimately follow. I just wanted my boys to know my sorrow, and they would know what I was talking about in each case without any elaboration. Before I was done I had written 18 pages of text and had apologized for 50 actions. I was shocked that I had been carrying that much regret in me; I felt much lighter just getting it all out.

I then had to transcribe it onto the computer so that it would be legible and because I needed a copy for each of the boys. Typed, the apology was 9 pages long. I decided to fax the letter to Sean but I had to send Jason's by mail. I knew that even if Sean refused to ever speak to me again, I would still have to send the letter to Jason just on principle alone. I was afraid that they would disown me, but then decided that if they did not leave me for the actions in the first place, why would they leave me when I apologized for doing them? Lucky for me at the time that I did not consider the reason they didn't leave was because they were just kids!

No matter what my thought process was before I sent it, when Sean did not call me back immediately and tell me that he had forgiven me a long time ago, I began to panic. I realized that not only did I want their forgiveness, I *expected* it. For some reason, I have never been able to do anything without preconceived ideas about how it is going to turn out. Maybe it is part of that "gotta be 10 steps ahead of everybody" scenario. Finally, after a number of hours, I called him to see if we were still OK. I could tell that he had been crying and my heart broke when he said, "Mom, you have to give me some time with this. It has brought back a lot of memories that I really didn't want to remember. For some reason, it makes it worse that you knew you did those things—they weren't as bad when I thought you just did them in a medicated haze. I need time."

After hearing that, I almost threw up, but I still had to send a copy to Jason. I sent it by mail and the same thing happened—when he did not get back to me after about a week, I called him. He said almost verbatim what Sean had said. I felt better, but it did not sound like they did at all. They both told me they forgave me, but they needed time to digest it all. I had to honor that, and I did.

When I got back to the lake, I told John that I had to burn the handwritten copy of my apology. That would be the only way it would really be out of my system. I put the 18 pages in a manila envelope and threw the whole thing into a raging bonfire. John and I watched as it burned. We were quite amazed at the process. Even though the fire was huge, the envelope did not burn right away. The top side burned first; for just a couple of seconds, the first page lay open in the flames, fully exposed and not burning at all. Then in a flash it was gone. This happened for every page; I was given time to have one more look at my words before they were gone forever. When the pages were all gone, only then did the back of the envelope, which was sitting directly in the fire, burn away. We could not believe it had not burned before then. It was an awe-inspiring few minutes and it was proof to me that I had done the right thing in sending it. The way my life changed on an inner level tells me it really is true that guilt stops growth. I just pray that my sons are also free now to do their own growing. Together, I think there is a good chance for all of us.

CHAPTER 20

In 1987, after being in lock-up and then being told that I was merely sad and not depressed, I checked myself out of the hospital, as mentioned earlier. That would be, thankfully, the last time I was hospitalized for depression. Somewhere in my very confused and fuzzy mind, I knew that I could not go there again. The fact that John only visited me twice during the last stay gave me a clue that he would not visit me ever again on a psychiatric ward. I knew that I would lose him and probably the kids if I let myself slide consciously into that pit again. On some very deep level, I had the wherewithal to know that I had a choice to make, which is very strange, because for four years, I thought that I was a victim of this disease and therefore had no say in any part of it.

I believe there is a payoff for any situation we stay in during our life—good situations or bad; it makes no difference. For instance, suppose I am in an honors program in college. I have the choice to stay or to quit. The payoff for me is that I am accomplishing something; I am feeling good about my marks; I am pleased with myself; my family is proud of me; I feel very hopeful about my future. The payoffs are great; so why would I bail out?

To choose to stay in a state of depression because there are payoffs sounds a little absurd, but people do it all the time.

Most will argue that they would never choose depression and they would vehemently declare that there certainly are not any payoffs. The *choice* to stay "down," even after their medications have been successful in clearing up their physical imbalances, is as common and as real as me sitting here writing this. I know, because I was guilty of it too. I believe now that five of my most obvious payoffs for staying "sick" were as follows:

I had no responsibilities because no one expected anything of me.

Other people were taking care of me instead of me taking care of them.

I no longer had to explain or justify my moods.

I did not have to do anything with money. John took over the finances.

And last, but not least, I did not have to pick weeds unless I wanted to! (You see I have learned to not take life so seriously!)

However, all of a sudden there was a price tag to pay to keep my "sickness" as an ongoing thing—I would lose my family. I had to decide which was bigger: the payoffs or the price. At first I refused to believe there were any payoffs, but as soon as I put them into my conscious mind, I realized they were very real. Once the subconscious behavior goes into the conscious realm, it becomes useless, powerless, and impossible to carry out—subconscious behavior is only possible when it is done subconsciously! At that point, to choose to stay in the world of mental illness was to mindfully choose to remain a victim. To choose to start making an exit was one of the first healthy and courageous actions that I had taken in a long time. This does not mean that I was miraculously fit as a fiddle. I know now that only after the decision to get well was made did the real work begin. I had to find doctors to help me, and admitting that I needed help was a healthy thing. As you know from earlier chapters it took me a while to find a truly healthy therapist, but persistence paid off. I eventually got the real deal when I found Dr. Radner.

As mentioned in the beginning, I voluntarily went off my medications in 1988 and I functioned reasonably well for the next 15 years. I had ups and downs, but as I had chosen to be well, I could not give those mood alterations much attention. During that time, I did not have the extremes that I had experienced before, so I just went with the flow. When I could not do that, I learned to manage my life around it. For instance, I worked with a wonderful friend and realtor named Reggie who picked up and delivered work to me at home so that I did not have to go out if I was having a bad day. That does not sound very healthy but it worked for about four years. It was not until we moved to Vancouver Island in 2003 that I was forced to seek medical help once more—I will talk about that later.

Depression is a very strange phenomenon because on one hand the depressed person has the self-esteem of a slug, but on the other hand that same person manages to get the whole world to revolve around him or her on a daily basis. I remember being totally self-centered, with everything being unquestionably just about *me*. The people closest to me tease me that I still think that way! I assure them that they are right, but unlike in my depressed years, now I do it with confidence and even some humor!! I spent so many years of my life in a nonexistent mode that it feels wonderful to acknowledge that I not only do indeed exist, but as the kids say today, "I rock!" As time goes on and after being called on it a few times, the pendulum is swinging to a healthy place somewhere in the middle of "I'm disappearing! I'm invisible" and "Look at me! I'm queen of the Universe!"

Coming from a person who has been there, I would caution families of clinically depressed people to not give more to your loved one, during his or her illness, than you gave when he or she was well. To dote on him or her makes the illness much more inviting than normal living is, and that becomes a pay-off for staying there. Care and compassion are healthy, but pampering and doting are quite the opposite. Clinical depression is an abnormality in the functioning of the chemicals of the brain, so *nobody* is to blame for it, not the patient and not the family. With that in mind, we must be aware that "guilt" cannot be the motive for the excessive outpouring of support. To really have the best interests of the depressed person in mind, I repeat, *Do not give more to your loved one, when ill, than you gave when he or she was well.*

I lost the ability to do many household chores because it took a lot of mental work and concentration to do even the smallest things. After a while, when the kids and John continued to do everything for me, I actually forgot how to do them and had to relearn a lot of ordinary things once I was on the road to recovery. Without a doubt, I was more pampered when I was ill than I ever was when I was well, and although that was done out of love, it was not in my best interests. My advice would be to expect some small task from your depressed loved one every day. To accomplish something builds self-esteem and confidence; it will make him or her feel better as well. Add small jobs every day (without making a big fuss about them) so that eventually, the person is back in the land of the living without realizing that the transition has been made. Doing nothing productive during those early months makes the road back to health much longer than it has to be.

There is no magic formula for coming out of the pit of depression and planting one's feet on solid ground once more.

If I had that formula, I would be a very rich woman. But I do know the things that have helped me along the way.

I have been very blessed in the fact that I have the awareness and the ability to listen to myself. I hear things in my mind (but no longer in an unhealthy way) and I listen. So often there are messages that I would have missed if I were to just push them away thinking they are unimportant. I have heard words of a song, or noticed a particular scene of a movie, or even unintentionally zeroed in on someone else's conversation, and I have recognized there is a message for me. When this happens the words seem louder than normal and it is as though no one else is even aware they are being said or seen.

Once I saw a movie where I heard one sentence that said exactly what I needed to hear that day: *The only pain you feel on the other side is the love you have withheld on this one*. The volume for that sentence was louder than the rest of the dialogue, and I thought at first that it was due to a fault in the soundtrack. Watching the movie again at a later date, I was surprised to hear those words were at the same volume as all the others. At that volume I would have completely missed the message if I had not known it was there. The next time I watched that movie (obviously a favorite of mine) I was dumbfounded when that line of the script was totally absent. I rewound the tape and went forward a few times, but the words that had meant so much to me were gone. I guess I had learned the lesson, so I did not need to hear them again.

I am a person who notices gifts as they are presented to me. Nothing is taken for granted and everything has meaning. I see teachings and learnings where many do not, and that is a fact. It is a part of who I am and it has accelerated my departure from the world of mental illness.

For instance, let me tell you about my dentures. Don't laugh! I realize that millions of people in this world have dentures, but I will guarantee that few of them learned from theirs what I did from mine. When I learned that I had to have my all top teeth removed, I became physically ill. I spent three days being sick to my stomach with no other symptoms so I do not believe I had the flu. Every step along the way to the day of the extractions was traumatic. Please know that I was not afraid of the procedure; I was going to be put to sleep so pain was not a part of this anxiety. The denturist could not believe the fear I had with just having the plaster images of my teeth made. The only way that I could describe it would be to say that I felt like I was grieving something or someone. Three days before the dastardly deed was to occur I was visiting Beth, and the fear that I was exhibiting was more than she felt she could help me with. She called my wonderful Dr. Radner, and miraculously, even with his busy schedule, he agreed to see me the next day. I went and told him my problem and he opened a wonderful door for me. We finally came to the conclusion that my teeth were symbolic of much more than the obvious.

I went home and did something that will make all of you think that I really am fooling myself if I think that I am now quite sane. The number of teeth that were being pulled was 13. So I wrote, on 13 pieces of paper, the characteristics of myself that I was willing to *let go of* at the time of the extractions, one for each tooth. I thought about them carefully, then I wrote down 13 things I wanted to come into my life to replace the negative traits that would be leaving. That weekend, John and I were at the lake; he lit a fire and we performed a ceremony. This is one of those times that I fell in love with him all over again; I know he was willing to take part in it just because it was important to me. His support at times like this makes me realize that I do, indeed, have a soft place to fall.

Standing beside the fire pit, I took each piece of paper and read out the "thing" I was giving up and what I was replacing it with; then I would throw that piece of paper into the fire. For instance, if I was willing to give up "LACK OF SELF-WORTH," then I would say that I was replacing it with "SELF-LOVE." As the flames ate up the piece of paper; the loss of that trait became reality. We watched the flames eat up the first 11 pieces of paper that represented the parts of my personality that I no longer needed. As I said, John was doing this because I believed it would do me good; however, in reality I think he thought it was a little far-fetched.

As skeptical as he was, John became a believer when the last two pieces would not burn even though I threw them right into the middle of the raging flames, just as I had done with all the others. Both papers jumped from the flames right out of the fire pit and landed on the grass two times each. John was the one who said, "I guess you aren't ready to give those things up yet." One of the papers read simply "FEAR." The other read "GUILT." On the third try, after saying a little prayer asking for help with them, they both succumbed to the flames, but I knew that I had much work to do in those areas.

As I said, for each item I gave up, I asked for something new and by the day of the surgery I was feeling quite calm. I knew that I had done some wonderful healing; as crazy as it sounds, it was just what I had needed. The whole dental procedure went without a hitch. The doctor told me later that he had seldom had such an easy time pulling teeth. He commented that the teeth came out very easily and that they must have been ready to go. If he only knew what those teeth stood for and just how ready they really were. The denturist said that I healed the fastest of anyone he had seen in a long time, commenting how I hardly had any bruising at all. My point is that many people have their teeth pulled, but I was one of the lucky ones who knew that even this very physical event had spiritual connections, so it became a part of my overall healing.

Marilyn Avient

CHAPTER 21

Accountability is a freeing concept, the learning of which did much to pull me out of that very familiar dark pit that I had dug for myself. To me, accountability equals power—not over anyone else, but rather personal inner power that gives you freedom and the ability to choose your own path in life.

Accountability is all about making choices. For the purpose of the next couple of pages, let's pretend that I have a job working in an office in the middle of a big city. From the moment I wake up in the morning I have choices to make. I choose whether to get out of bed or not. My next choice always has to do with whether I am going let fear be an active part of my day or not. How I handle that choice often indicates how I am going to manage the rest of my day. I choose whether to smile or frown. I choose whether I am going to brush my teeth and shower or not. I can choose what color I am going to wear, and this is a visible indicator of the other choices I am making for that day. (Choosing bright colored clothes would indicate the likelihood of making positive choices that day.) I can choose to do things that will slow me down and therefore put me at risk of being late for work, or I can give myself an extra five minutes and go calmly out the door. I can choose how to react to the fact that that my husband did not take out the garbage as I had asked him to do the night before.

As I am driving, I can choose what speeds I am going to travel, what routes I am going to take, and how I am going to react to the other drivers as they make own their choices. When I get to work I can choose to cheerfully acknowledge my co-workers, or I can ignore them and be rude. I can choose how I am going to respond to authority figures outwardly as well as inside of myself. When my phone rings, I can choose to smile and greet the caller enthusiastically, or I can be cold and businesslike. I can choose how to meet and greet clients. I can choose whether to eat something healthy or something fattening for lunch. I can choose to call my husband and tell him I love him or I can call him and let him have it for not taking out that darned garbage. There is barely a minute in the day when there is an absence of choices to be made.

When I get home in the late afternoon, the choice-making continues. When asked how my day was, I can choose to say that it was wonderful, boring, or horrible. I can choose whether to take responsibility for my day or blame it on the world—the traffic was terrible, the girls at the office all had PMS, the boss is impossible to please, the cop who gave me the speeding ticket should be shot. The traffic may have been heavier than usual. The girls may have been reacting to my bad mood. The boss may be under a great deal of pressure from other corners. I chose to speed and so deserved the ticket—the police officer was just doing his job.

At night, when I go to bed, I have the choice to lie there and give thanks for all the lessons I have received that day or I can lie there in dread of waking up and going through it all again. I could say "Thank God, this day is over!" or else "Thank you, God, for this day that's over."

At night, I have learned to look back and give thanks for at least five things that happened during my day. I say thank you for the things—some good and some not so good—that provided me lessons. I think of it this way: I operate much better when people around me say thank you for things that I have done; they make me feel good. I bet God feels the same way! Try it.

As small as those items all appear to be, their sum equals *one day in my life*. It is a day I cannot have over again. There are no chances to go back to fix it up and make it right—there are no do-overs in life. Sure I get another chance the next day, but so often we do not learn from the past; that rule seems to apply even on a day-to-day basis.

I have talked about choices in a single ordinary day and none of them are earthshaking, but each one is necessary at the moment that we make it. Another way to say it is that a day is nothing more than the sum of our choices during one 24-hour period! Every reaction that we make about every other person we meet and every event in which we participate becomes ingrained in us; we use each reaction as a reference the next time that same kind of event occurs. We are creatures of habit and that does not add to our growth at all.

If you want to have a fun day, try reacting differently to everything that comes your way. When the phone rings, do not answer. When someone honks at you in traffic, wave and smile warmly. When someone tells you that you are less than wonderful, express your thanks for the feedback. If you are normally a positive person, just for the learning, try choosing a response that is not so positive. It is important for you to know that you have choices in every little seemingly insignificant part of your day. There are no set responses to any given event, so choose to react in a way that feels good, deep inside of you; do not be swayed by what you chose to do last time.

Then there are the choices that change lives—the big ones. Through all my growing up years, I dreamed of becoming a nurse. I had a cousin who was in nurses' training at one of the city hospitals; when we would take her back to residence, after a weekend with us, I remember crying because I envied her so much. I could not wait to be there myself. That dream lasted until the day it was possible to start making it come true.

In the middle of grade 12, I knew that I had to put in applications for my training. My parents were open to whatever I chose to take, so there was no pressure from them. When my dad asked me what I was going to do, I could hardly believe my ears when I heard myself telling him that I was going to go to the Northern Alberta Institute of Technology (NAIT) to become a medical laboratory technologist. Before that day, I had not even considered that as a career choice, but without any thought I committed myself to taking the two-year course. Would you believe nursing was never mentioned in our house again? No one questioned me about my change of heart, and I just let myself start walking down that well-trodden path of least resistance. You may be wondering what happened to change my mind like that!

What happened is that I took the easy way out as I so often did when fear was involved. I began to realize that nurses do some very scary, very responsible things that I did not think I was capable of doing. I figured that I would be safe as a technologist because in those days labs were always located in basements and they rarely had any windows. I would be hidden and no one would ever see if I was less than efficient at this work. Think about it—how could anything very important originate from a windowless room in a basement? Funny that I never even considered that people's lives are in the hands of lab technicians every day! Funny that I failed to realize that all the medical breakthroughs through all the years have come from laboratories and it did not matter one iota how many windows were there.

Also, in 1968, nursing was a three-year course in which you had to live in residence, and I knew that I could not handle that (you know, that "I'm scared to be away from home" kind of fearful thinking). Dan and I were talking about marriage and three years was too long to wait. Lab technology was only a two-year course and I could stay at home the whole time. I remember telling someone that I was only getting an education in case something happened to Dan after we got married. That was the typical thinking of married women who had not yet become a part of the feminist movement; in this case it would turn out to be a premonition of things to come!

I went into lab training and, oh, how I hated it! I got excellent marks because I studied very hard, but the hospital training almost did me in. Now I realize that I probably would have had trouble with the nurses' training, too, but at least my heart would have been in it. I went home crying almost every day. Once, even though I followed the accepted protocol, I was involved in an incident in which a doctor misinterpreted my findings and a patient almost died. (So much for nothing important ever happening in windowless basements!) I remember one night working all alone in the chemistry lab, lying down on the floor doubled up with a stress-related stomachache. When I was finished my training I chose to work in a private lab because I could not take the constant stress of the hospital scene.

I made a choice, but I made it out of fear, so it could not be anything but traumatic. I would have been a wonderful nurse, but I was too afraid to try; instead, I made up excuses to get myself off the hook so that I did not even have to attempt the challenge. However, that said, I did make a choice, and I did live with the consequences, and I am grateful to the Universe for the lessons that I learned along the way. For that reason, I do not regret the decision I made that day, but I do sometimes wonder what my life would have been like if I had been brave enough to choose to follow my dream.

We often forget, when we think about the glory of creating our life through making choices, that for every choice we make, there is a direct and fitting consequence. Our whole society is built on actions and reactions or choices and consequences—just take a look at the criminal system. The strange thing is that people know the undesirable consequences, but they go ahead and do the causative act anyway.

I made some choices that had terrible consequences. I told you in an earlier chapter about my behavior during my first marriage and before my marriage to John. Even though Dan and I were both in the marriage, I am responsible for my part in its demise, so I will not talk about his role at all. I committed adultery and that played a big role in our breakup. Adults performed the actions and the children did the suffering—action/reaction. Sean and Jason did not deserve the heartbreak that they went through; they had to grow up so fast that it must have made an observer wonder just who were the adults and who were the children.

I am so sorry that my two darling boys had to feel the pain that they did; you may think they were too young to grasp what was happening, but trust me, they suffered. Some people said that because the children were so little, Dan and I could each take one and they would not even notice. But that would have killed them, especially Jason, as the only person he trusted was Sean; he clung to him every minute of the day. The nights I held them as they cried themselves to sleep because they missed their father are just too sad to think about. And then I made the choice to be out almost every night partying like a fool while my children were at home frightened that they were going to lose me too. I acted foolishly and ignorantly and my babies suffered. Luckily, I finally made a good decision when I married John, so my children were blessed with another good man in their lives. John has always been a wonderful dad to them and, in his mind, they are his sons. So now they have a good *father* as well as a good *dad*.

People cringe at the word *responsibility*, but it is nothing to back away from. In fact, knowing that I am responsible for everything in my life gives me comfort, strength, and power. There is no glory in being a victim and that is what you become when you let the world make your choices for you, when you feel you have none. For instance, you have all heard the saying that the only things you can count on in life are death and taxes. So you cannot possibly have any choice in them. Wrong! You choose to live in a free and beautiful country; paying taxes is one of the conditions that come with the package. You may think that you have no choice about dying, but whether you believe it or not you did choose to live; consequently, you have also chosen to die.

Many years ago I was listening to a motivational tape and the speaker dissected the word *responsibility*. What he said stayed with me and so I made it part of my learning process. *Responsibility* can be dissected into *response-ability*, or the "ability to respond." That means you have the ability to make any situation into anything that you choose. This is a *power* statement. Even if you are in a car accident you may choose to be a victim, especially if, by law, it is the other person's fault. However, no matter what the law says, if you merely utter the words "Why did I need this lesson?" or "What lessons have I set up for myself in this accident?" you will feel yourself rising to a place within you that literally gives you power over your whole world. Realizing you have the "ability to respond" to absolutely everything you do automatically makes you as powerful as the Universe intends you to be.

I have made the amazing discovery that, despite what many people think, the Universe is benevolent and truly wants me (all of us) to succeed. You hear people say they are doomed for failure or that the whole world is against them. If that is the way it is for them, it is because they have chosen through their thoughts and actions to make it so. I merely have to choose to triumph over all the adversities and challenges that come my way, and I do. If I am *accountable* for each of my life's situations, and see them as **lessons instead of problems**, then my life immediately becomes beautiful in ways that are beyond my wildest dreams.

I have found that when I feel depressed, it is better to just feel it, embrace it, and go through it, instead of groveling in it—or running from it—the way that I did in the past. Sometimes, when I wake up with that familiar black cloud hanging over my bed, I say something to the effect of "OK, today I feel like crap so I am going to let myself feel this way for 24 hours. Tomorrow morning I will wake up feeling cheerful and at peace with the world." And so begins my day of feeling sad and sorry for myself, but nine times out of ten, I get tired of it much sooner than 24 hours later. Often, by noon, I am starting to snap out of it and by 2 pm I find myself being productive. Giving myself permission to feel those bad feelings immediately stops me from becoming a victim. I have even been told that *when we feel the most out of control, that is when we are being taken care of the most.* That is when we have the most opportunity to learn and grow.

CHAPTER 22

I believe in miracles!

Miracles prove to me that there is a Higher Power who makes sure that I see beyond all that is mundane in my life. To me, a miracle occurs when God personally answers a prayer even though I may not know that I have prayed it. It is a moment when the veil that divides this world and the next ruffles a little in the wind and the line between is not so clear-cut anymore.

I *expect miracles, and so I get them!* Yes, it is just that easy! Life truly is as simple as getting my *needs* met—this is a long way from *getting your own way* or getting everything you *want*. Miracles are wonderful ways to get the proof we all need to show us that there really is a point to having faith. Acknowledging miracles, as a reality, has done much to lessen the number of days that I have had to confront that constant and powerful black cloud. Actually most miracles are simple and only recognizable by people who have the faith to believe in them. Some people say that *seeing is believing*; others of us think that it is more of a case of *believing is seeing*. One of the miracles that I did not immediately recognize, as such, was very simple and yet very complex.

I went to a channeler/reader in 2003 and I came away

feeling very good about the world in general, and my life in particular. Among other things, she told me to always ask God for what I *need* and never for what I *wish, desire, or want.* I told her that I did not want to appear needy to anyone—especially not to God; I would rather say that I desire something as opposed to needing it. She said, "If you think that you should not ask for what you need, then tell me what you need." I thought about it for a moment and then I told her that there was nothing that I needed! She smiled mischievously, saying, "See, it works! We really do get everything we *need.*" So from that day on, when I have needed help in some way, that is exactly what I pray for, "Dear God, I *need* [something]," and I always get it. So now, to me, *need* is a magic word. That may not seem like a miracle, but it changed my life, so what else would you call it?

I related to you the miracle that happened during my 1987 stay in hospital when I ran head on into "Jesus." That day I was used as a channel, and that will be one of those things that I will remember and cherish on my deathbed. There is another event that I consider a miracle that changed the depth of my spiritual beliefs and, as is so often the case, it came to me in the form of something very simple. I call it my "English Ivy story."

Towards the end of 1976, I bought a tiny English Ivy plant. I watered it, talked to it, and lovingly watched it for signs of growth. I saw nothing. John, with whom I was living at the time, said that he would take this plant, which had refused to thrive for me, to his office where he would pamper it into growing. After a few months he brought it home, and proudly showed me my ivy, which had grown at least six feet in that a very short time. (Sometimes I have wondered if he went out and bought a fully grown one just so that he could show me what a wonder he was!) Believe me, I was mighty impressed with the green thumb that my husband-to-be apparently had. I immediately set the vast mass of leaves up on a shelf in the sunniest window and promptly forgot about it.

My lack of attention was not intentional. I was very busy organizing our wedding—doing all the cooking, baking, sewing, and planning. At the same time I was upset and worried about my father, who was dying. My emotions were in a highly confused state. Plants were thus not a high priority.

One day a few weeks before the wedding, I looked up at the plant and saw that the combination of hot sun and no water had fried it to a crisp brown. John, who was out of town working, was totally unaware of what I had done to his beautiful ivy. I berated myself for being so apathetic over something that supposedly meant a lot to me. I immediately took it down from the shelf and cut off the brown array of leaves so that only six inches of the dead stem remained. I was going to throw it out, but being the sentimental fool that I am, I placed the pot, filled with dirt containing the dead stem, high up on a shelf in the living room. Needless to say, John was not too happy when he came home and saw what I had done to his one victory in the plant kingdom. Come to think of it, he has never tried to grow a plant since!

However, the plant was again forgotten in our fluster of activity and our emotions that ran the gamut from excitement about our big day to sorrow and worry about Dad. In 1974, my parents did their one rebellious thing in life and moved to Vancouver Island without asking any of us kids for input. Dad was in the latter stages of emphysema and living at sea level was good for him.

Our wedding was planned for March 19, 1977. Around the

first of March, Mom called, saying it would be a good idea for us to come to the coast immediately. My brother, Dave, and I headed out there to say our last good-byes and to give Mom our support. On the morning of our first day back, I went to the cemetery and picked out a plot for my father. In the afternoon I picked up the ham and turkey for our wedding celebration. I did not know whether to laugh or cry, so I cried, mostly about the impending death of my beloved father, but also because it did not seem fair that my wedding had to be planned with this dark and ugly cloud lurking menacingly on the horizon.

A week before the wedding I awoke feeling better than I had in weeks. I told John that I had just had a dream in which my dad had appeared and told me that he had no plans of going anywhere until after our wedding. Within minutes of telling John this, Mom phoned to say Dad had taken a turn for the better; in fact, he was sitting up in bed and talking quite lucidly for the first time in a long while. I told her that I already knew this and then told her about my dream. I never worried again about him leaving this earth before my wedding day.

The wedding day came and went. As promised, my Dad lived on. The aftermath of the wedding was a nightmare for me because I was exhausted from the myriad of emotions that had been with me on a daily basis for weeks. I was so wiped out that I could hardly stay awake for more than a few hours at a time. April arrived and my stamina thankfully returned. Dad was still alive and life was looking quite promising for me, the new bride. Looking back, I can see the logic of the Universe. My strength was being restored so that I could deal with the stress of the sorrow that was to come.

Thankfully I had that renewed strength because in spite of

knowing what was coming, my world fell apart when Mom called on April 14 to say that Dad was gone. The only way that I could face the shock was to delve headfirst into the details of arranging the funeral. I took care of Mom, cooked many meals for my family, helped Mom plan the funeral, and gave a very brief eulogy at the funeral. As long as I was busy with the details of getting Dad buried, I did not need to deal with the fact that he was dead.

By this time, we were living in a high-rise apartment on the southwest side of Edmonton that we moved into only a few months after John and I met. The tiny townhouse on the other side of town that I lived in with the boys was too small and far away from everything, and it held too many memories of my days as a party girl. We stayed in this 10th floor apartment until we moved into our house at South Cooking Lake 18 months later.

After Mom and my sister Barbara had gone home, I was left with the emptiness that always occurs following the death of someone so dear. One night when John was away working and the children were asleep, I remember standing in front of my patio doors, looking out over the city from our balcony, and asking Dad to please show me that he was still near to me. As I looked out at the dark night, I could feel his presence, but I could not see him, and I wondered just where he was.

A few days later, John came home for the weekend. The first night he was home, we chose to stay in and watch television, because he was tired and I was in no mood to do anything else. At some point in the evening, John turned his head, looked up to the top shelf, and casually said, "I see that you've been watering our ivy again. Boy, those leaves are sure bigger than the original ones." I looked up to see what he was talking about and declared that I had not given the plant any thought, let alone any water, in months. When my mind finally registered what my eyes were reluctant to see, I realized that I had gotten the sign that I had asked for from my Dad!

Without a word of a lie, the brown, crisp stem had six huge, green, lush leaves on it. They were fully grown and looked out of place on the dead stem, which was standing in dirt that was cracked and hard as cement. We took it down and examined it. I reiterated to John that this was my Dad telling me that he was close by. John looked at me like I was crazy, but he admitted that he did not have a better explanation.

As we lovingly watered the strange spectacle, I kept thinking that by giving this plant a second chance, my Dad was actually saying that I should pick up my life and live, instead of constantly focusing on his death. Before watering the ivy, we placed the pot on a saucer to catch the excess water and then left it on the table where it stayed until morning.

When we got up and looked at our "baby," we were incredulous to see that the leaves were gone without a trace, and the dead stem was once more sitting in cracked, hard soil. There was no evidence that we had given it even one drop of water. The saucer was completely dry, whereas last night the bottom of it was covered in water. Everything had returned to its previous state. When John saw the transformation, he said, "Now, *that* is your dad speaking!" He said the disappearance of the leaves was more remarkable to him than the appearance of them. Me, I thought it was all pretty darned amazing!

To this day, there is not a question in my mind as to the cause of those mysterious events. This plant played a very important role in my life and it lived the exact life that it was supposed to so that it could be used as a vessel of learning for the message to me from my beloved father. My dad spoke and, as I had done throughout my childhood, I listened.

Another, yet very different, miracle happened in 2001 and this time *water* was the conduit that God used to teach me a lesson, even if that lesson was no more than a reminder of his loving power. This story is about a flooding basement.

In December of 2000 we bought a beautiful house that had formerly been a show home. We had lived in the rental condo (after South Cooking Lake) from 1988 to 1992 and then bought a condo where lived until we bought this brand new home. Buying something so new, we never expected any problems, and I will admit that we were a little too house-proud. This happened in July 2001 during the heaviest downpour that year.

We had friends over the night of the big rainstorm, and they had to go home early because they were concerned about their basement flooding. We were not worried because we knew our new house had no problems, so we went to bed without even checking the basement. The next morning the dogs went downstairs. When I noticed them licking the rug, I went to see why. I felt moisture in the rug through my socks. There was a ring of water in the family room that extended out about six feet from the wall that separated that room from the furnace room. My office also had a wet area that came out about the same distance.

John checked things out and discovered that our sump pump was not working. He tried bailing a little water out of the sump area, but it did little except to make him *feel* like he was doing something. We went upstairs and ate breakfast— believe it or not. We were in the middle of a huge calamity, yet we calmly decided to eat a big breakfast. That took about 20 minutes. John then left to find a new pump and a vacuum cleaner to suck up the water from the rug. All that calmness was just *so* out of my character that it should have been our first clue that this situation was more than it appeared.

While he was gone, I went downstairs with a jug to bail out water from the holding tank. I poured the water down the drain in the floor and I could hear it going down quite noisily. When I was not pouring, there was no noise of water running, so I had to assume that no water was running from the floor down the drain on its own. I was feeling sick—my beautiful house was drowning; I was in the midst of one of my worst nightmares. However, as I bailed out one jugful at a time—it did not seem to be making any difference whatsoever —I started asking myself questions like "What is the lesson that I am meant to learn from this?" I wondered why I had brought this catastrophe into my life. I sat there thinking while my arm kept filling the jug, emptying the jug, filling the jug, emptying the jug. I noticed that light appeared to be streaming through the window and onto me in the shape of a V. I felt an unfamiliar yet beautiful calm come over me as I bathed in its warm light. As I sat there safely enclosed in the beam of light I was reminded of this same occurrence at the seminar in 1999.

I looked out that same window and saw my neighbor digging a trench to redirect the water on the side of her house, so I went outside and just said, "Hi, Linda. You're doing a good job and you're not alone." I went back in and did a little more useless bailing until John returned. He had all the gadgets and gizmos necessary to fix the situation, so I stopped bailing. (That in itself was a miracle because houses were flooding all over the city and the hardware stores never have enough pumps and vacuums in stock in such major situations.) It took him a while to get organized, but finally he was ready to pump out the tank that was full to the brim. It was still pouring outside. In the meantime, I was examining the family room rug and it had no more water in it than when we had first noticed it.

When John got the tank emptied he called me to show me the water pouring in from outside. The pipe that led into the sump tank was about three inches across and the water was pouring in at full tilt. John told me that it was coming in at a rate of about two gallons per minute. All this information fell on deaf ears because anything mechanical is quite beyond me and so, to feel useful, I started vacuuming up the water in the family room. The line of demarcation had not moved—still about six feet out. We worked for hours that day and the next. I put down towels, picked them up, and put them in the dryer. I did this over and over and over again for three days.

Finally, the rugs were dry. To our amazement, there were no water stains showing where the moisture had been. There was no musty smell in the basement as so often happens after a flood. In essence, there was no sign that anything had happened at all. John had bought an extra pump so that we would never be caught unprepared again and we both went back to normalcy, feeling grateful that the damage had been quite minor compared to the many damaged houses throughout the city.

Three nights later, I was almost asleep when I bolted up in bed. John asked what was wrong and I said, "John, where did all that water go?" He asked, "What water?" I continued, "The two gallons a minute that was pouring into our basement. I was not able to take out that much and for part of the time, nobody was bailing out at all—like when we were upstairs leisurely eating breakfast. At two gallons per minute, there should have been 60 gallons of water on the rugs just while we were eating. I don't even know what possessed us to eat breakfast when we knew our basement was filling with water." John thought for a moment, and said, "Well, the drain was probably taking it away." I told him that I had listened for water running down the drain when I was not pouring it down and I heard none running at all. After a few minutes he slowly said, "At the rate it was pouring in, our *whole* basement should have been under at least six inches of water. You're right! The water did not move at all from the time we discovered the rug was wet until I got the pump changed and the tank vacuumed out. I don't know where the water went."

I went on to tell him about the light flooding in the window in a huge V shape. It had been pouring rain all day—the sun had not been out at all. I related to John that I felt the most amazing peace while the light was shining on me. Even the way I spoke to the neighbor had been very out of character. I wonder what she thought about me telling her that *she was not alone.* The more John and I talked, the more I knew that we were participants in a miracle. I also believe our calmness and my willingness to accept responsibility for it as a life lesson changed a potentially miserable situation into a blessing straight from God. In essence, I lived some of my favorite words: *When you seek the perfection in a moment of despair, it transforms into a moment of grace.* No doubt about it; that is what I believe happened to me. I thank God for the experience and the reminder of his presence in my life.

Here is another miracle that happened to us, which I believe is an example of guardian angels stepping in to prevent premature death: One day John and I were driving down an avenue in Edmonton that was intersected by a street with a stop sign, thereby giving us the right of way. I was the driver. I was just about at the intersection; I could not see any traffic— in fact, it is a hidden corner. I had driven down this avenue many times before and had never had any trepidation about that corner. However, this time without any provocation, before I got to the spot where I *could* see anything coming, I stopped the car. In amazement, and with probably a little annoyance at me for being a "typical woman driver," John said, "Why'd you stop?" Suddenly a car came storming down the intersecting street and went right through the stop sign crossing in front of us at a speed far exceeding the legal limit. As he flew past us, I answered John, "Because of that!" with my head following the movement of the speeding car as I spoke. John asked me how I knew it was coming. I told him that I had no idea. The car had not been visible; I experienced no conscious thoughts about stopping; I did not hear anything—I just stopped.

I know beyond a shadow of a doubt that my guardian angel made my car stop because it was not my time to die, nor was it John's. My car just came to a halt. I did not feel like I had any part in making it stop, nor in the decision making that preceded it. I totally believe the car was made to stop because if it had not, one or both of us would have died and that, apparently, was not meant to be. Guardian angels will never let you die ahead of your time, unless, of course, it is by your own hand and that brings about all sorts of other lessons.

I would like to share with you an event that happened to my father in the 1950s. Dad was in the army and earned just under $200 per month. The mortgage payment was $98, leaving about $100 for food for five people (when Dad was away) and all the other expenses. Dad was posted in an army facility far from where we lived and was absent for weeks at a time. On this particular day, he had been home on a weekend pass and had to return to work by train on Sunday night. He had just gotten paid, but it was a tight month, so he gave Mom all of the money, telling her that he had enough to get him through the weeks until next payday. In reality, he did not have a penny to his name. Just as he was going to step up into the train, he saw a $5 bill just lying there on the platform beside him. Other people had passed it but no one picked it up. He had the feeling that no one else could see it but him. This may not seem like much to us now, but then it was 1/20 of his monthly pay and it was enough to cover his expenses, including cigarettes, for the whole time that he would be away. To him it was a miracle. I suspect he was being rewarded for his unselfishness and for thinking of Mom before he thought of himself.

Some miracles help us to see that we are on the right path. One incident involving my mother did just that. In 1981, John was invited to become a partner in the large engineering and oil field construction firm that he worked for. The only catch was that he had to purchase some mandatory shares to the tune of $21,000—we did not even have $21 in savings! John and I were sitting at the table feeling very sad because although our credit was maximized with two mortgages, we knew that this was the opportunity of a lifetime. John had talked to the banks, but to no avail because of our heavy debt load.

As we were sitting there lamenting and worrying, my mother pulled into the driveway. She asked John if she could talk to him alone, so he went outside with her. She told him that she needed some financial advice. (I am not sure why she did not want to talk about it in front of me!) Mom said she had an investment that was maturing and she had to decide whether to cash it out or reinvest it for another five years. She wondered if John had any idea where she could invest the money so that it would accumulate more interest than she had been receiving. John, of course, asked how much money she was talking about and almost fell over when she replied, "$21,000." Trying to sound cool, he nervously cleared his throat, and then asked her if she would be willing to take a chance and invest in him. She said that she would if we would pay her the interest she required. John agreed and a contract was drawn up. We invested the money in the company and now 25 years later we are living on the very abundant fruits of that original investment. Mom was an astute businesswoman; every year she examined the interest rates and every year we paid what she asked. After all, she had saved our butts and for that we have always been grateful. We were undoubtedly the best investment that Mom ever made—in 10 years we paid her $35,000! When she realized that, she cancelled the loan.

The final miracle that I will relate to you is about my dad's funeral and some events that followed. When Mom called to say that Dad had passed away, she told me that she would be accompanying Dad's body back to Edmonton by plane and arriving the following night. Since moving out to the coast three years earlier, in 1974, Dad had never come home for a visit and somehow it really shook me to think of him coming back this way—in a box! I really cannot imagine how my mother survived that flight knowing that Dad was in the cargo area. That thought gives me a shiver even now.

My dad spent many hours of his day writing both prose and poetry, so I thought it would be only fitting that one of his poems be read at his funeral. Of course, I could not stand the thought of anyone other than myself reading the selected verses, so I decided that I would do this task as a last tribute to this man whom I had adored for all of my life. Mom, knowing how very emotional I was, worried about me having to stand up and address his death in public, but for me that was easier to focus on, than the fact that he was gone.

The ride to the funeral home in the long black limousine was awesome. I felt like I was in a dream and this was all one big fantasy from which I could awake at my leisure. Years ago, it was tradition that when a funeral procession went by, everything and everyone stopped what they were doing to show respect to the person who had died, as well as to the grieving relatives. Traffic would not move until the whole funeral procession had gone by—it was even allowed to go through red lights. However, by 1977, with the vast growth of cities, this practice had pretty well disappeared. That is why I was so very touched when I saw an elderly gentleman, who was walking along the street, stop, take off his hat, and hold it over his heart as we passed. I knew my dad would have liked that because he would have done the same thing himself. Throughout his life, Dad had probably shown this kind of tribute many, many times. I shall never forget that man and I hope that when he died, someone showed him that same respect.

THE OLD MAN

April, a sunny day, crowded streets.
Lunch hour is over. Workers hurry.
For them, an ordinary day.
A snake with all its eyes lit up follows,
As though mesmerized,
Two black, shiny cars. Slowly moving,
Purposefully moving, block by miserable block.
One black car full of people. Sad people,
Blank and staring people.
Looking, but not seeing.

For them, no street exists.
Second black car. One long oak box. A loved one.
Some heart is breaking.
Could be your relative.
Could be mine. Could be you. Could be me.
On a street corner, same as the rest,
An old man stands. Looking, waiting.
As the oak box passes, his hat comes off,
His hand goes to his heart,
He bows his head.
His quiet act of homage stands out loudly.
Noisy workers are quiet in comparison.
This old man had lived long,
Had felt Death, knew the pain.
He respected Death for soon it would be his.
Only one girl in the long black car
Saw the old man.
Her only remembrance of that special day
When slowly they drove
To fill her father's freshly dug grave.

Ten years have passed since that day,
And only the memory of a man on the corner,
Paying respects,
Makes her really believe that her dad is dead.
Just one old man, hand to heart, brings pain.
But now, at least, she waits no more.

When we got to the church I went to the back room, where
I waited until it was time to go into the chapel with the min-

ister. As I waited, my mouth felt like it was filled with cotton balls. I prayed to God to let me relax long enough to pay homage to my father. Immediately, I calmed down; the cotton balls disappeared. I knew that I would be fine. As I walked out into the chapel, I saw the long brown box covered in flowers, which earlier had upset me. Now, however, it looked quite harmless. I knew in my heart of hearts that my dad was not in that box, that it merely held his earthly remains. As confirmation, I felt a warm hand on my right shoulder and I felt, rather than heard, the words, "Don't worry, Darling, I am with you always!" My confidence soared and I stepped up to do this privileged deed.

I am sure the congregation was as shocked as I was that I was up there smiling. At that moment, knowing that my dad was closer to me than he had ever been before, I was beside myself with joy. By his words, Dad had told me that his spirit was nearby and I know that confirmation made my spiritual quest advance just a little faster. Only then did I know for sure that there was life after death. That was a revelation indeed. (Weeks later, this would be reconfirmed with the English Ivy.) As I spoke and read Dad's poem, I saw people smiling up at me. That was a wonderful feeling because that was a sure sign they had received some of the joy I was feeling.

That was the last day that I would know joy for a very long time. Somehow, I got lost in the dregs of mourning, refusing to believe Dad had really gone. John wondered where his happy little bride had disappeared to, and he had every right to be concerned. The wondrous happenings in the pulpit that day might just as well have happened to someone else for all the good they did me in the subsequent years. I actually just put them out of my mind, and chose to fall into the depths where I felt comfortable. My grieving was ongoing and unhealthy, to say the least!

The unresolved grieving varied in velocity for many years. In about 1982, a friend of mine from work persuaded me to go to a clairvoyant psychic with her. I went and was glad that I did. The psychic asked me to give her my wedding ring. Almost as soon as she touched it she started to see images. She saw some interesting guides around me, but before she had time to elaborate, she started to cough, choke, and gasp for breath.

When she finally settled down, she told me that someone very close to me had died from a suffocating lung condition, and that his death had been a real shock to me. I told her that my dad had died of emphysema, but that his death had been expected for a long time so it was definitely not a shock. She just looked at me and said, "You may have been expecting it, but you went into a shock so severe that you are still not out of it." At that point, I really began to listen to her.

She then said, "There is an elderly gentleman standing behind you and he has his hand on your right shoulder. He has a message for you. He wants me to tell you that *you are not to worry because he is with you always.*" At that point, I, too, almost started to choke as I told her that was exactly what happened as I stood at the pulpit at Dad's funeral. Again, my father's spiritual presence had been confirmed and I knew that he was trying to remind me, this time through this woman, that I was never alone and that I had a life to live. Once more, I marveled at the event, but refused to bring the meaning into my life.

By March of 1984, I was in my depression. I felt that I had no reason to live and wished that I were dead. Thinking that maybe I just needed a break from work, I went to Calgary with

John where he was doing a job. You may remember that I mentioned this trip earlier as part of the lead-up to my collapse. I thought a week's rest would do me good, but it did not; even the evenings with John did nothing to lift my spirits. One day I went for a walk, ending up in a small shopping mall where a flea market was being held. I saw a tarot card reader who only charged $5.00, so I asked her for a reading. I was only mildly impressed. What she mainly did was confirm that my depression was very real, and that I was in for a bit of a rough time in the coming months or even years.

I thanked the woman and walked away. I got about 50 feet away from her when she came running after me. She said, "Did you know that you have an elderly gentleman walking with you on your right side? He says that *you are not to worry and that he is with you always.*" I could not believe my ears. This message had been given to me three times, so you would think that I would have the sense to believe it. In my depressed state of mind, the only conclusion that I came to was that I would never go to a psychic again. I cannot remember why it was so difficult for me to believe my father was with me and would always take care of me. I never forgot the words, but until I got past my days of deep depression, I did not value and appreciate them.

The darkening shadows were closing in. As I walked away from that woman, I had no idea of the mental pain that was to be mine very soon. I wonder how my life would have been different if I had chosen to embrace my dad's message and draw comfort from it rather than running away from it. I will never know the answer to that. Obviously, it was necessary for me to ignore it so that I could, indeed, experience the whole process of my life. I did not know it then, but that was the beginning of the end of the "me" that had been in existence for the first

36 years of my life.

So, you see, miracles happen in all sorts of ways to all sorts of people for all kinds of different reasons. To me, miracles make the world go around. They make the mundane bearable and the heavy load light. A miracle is anything that makes you ponder the existence of a higher power. A miracle can be as down to earth as unexpectedly finding something that was lost or as heaven-sent as two tiny cells joining together to grow into a perfectly assembled tiny person in only nine short months. Think of the rose that starts out as a tiny bud and then one morning opens up into what I can only say is *the definition of beauty*. Think of the totally unremarkable cocoon that turns into one of God's best works—the butterfly. Think of the delight of a rainbow that shows us there can be beauty and light after any storm. Think of a sunset as it majestically closes the day with peace and grace. And what about a sunrise that quietly heralds a brand new day, thereby giving us another chance to get it right? If God can do all those amazing things in nature, imagine what he can and does do for each of us every single day of our lives. All we have to do is to be willing to take notice. Remember, when it comes to miracles—*I expect them; so I get them.* It just doesn't get any simpler than that.

CHAPTER 23

Since my breakdown I have delved deep into my soul and have learned a lot. I am grateful that my breakdown made me look inside—and outside—to find the answers that would allow me to grow on all levels. There are three little words that really make sense to me and have given me peace more times than you can ever know. Those words are *trust the process*. The miracles in the last chapter are fine examples that there is something happening that is out of our control, and when we dare to let ourselves see and hear the messages that accompany these awe-inspiring occurrences, the results are nothing less than amazing.

To me, life is like a river and I (as do all of us) have a choice of whether to go upstream or go down. I can go with the flow of my river, and I know that once in a while I will bump up against a rock, but life will move me past it. I will most likely have to dodge a hanging branch now and then, and on those occasions, I will merely bend to miss it and soon the branch will not be an issue anymore. I can even get washed to shore on occasions, and when I do, I know that I am meant to stop and rest a while. Sometimes a waterfall will loom ahead of me, and then I know that I am in for a wild ride. I have the choice at that point to safely get out and walk along the shore, or I can have faith that I will be taken care of by the Force that is bigger and more in tune with the purpose of my life than I am. Sometimes the river flows without a ripple so the going is easy and uneventful. That is the time to just *be* and trust that I am being given some rest in preparation for whatever is around the next bend.

I have not always chosen to go with the flow of my life. I have gone against the tide for much of my existence. I wanted to do it my way and wondered why I never got anywhere as I struggled to climb *up* the waterfalls and over the slippery rocks. I never got a chance to rest on shore because I was too busy battling the water and trying to just stay afloat. Then there were those many, many days when I let myself be swallowed up by the quicksand that lies along the some of the edges of the river of my life. On those days, I realize that I did not fight very hard to keep my head above water. But in the end it was plain old-fashioned hard work that totally defeated me. Because I was fighting Life itself, I never was allowed a glimpse at my purpose. To illustrate, this I wrote the following poem in about the year 1989.

AGAINST THE TIDE

The waters of the river flow
So naturally to the sea.
This plan of Nature says, "Start small,
Then grow as big as you can be."
Who is Mother Nature anyway
And why is she so smart?
My plans are born as big as oceans
And there my journey starts.
I jump into my leaky boat

And paddle fiercely against the tide.
I, soon, am discouraged and weary,
My boat gets tossed from side to side.
Not long, I see I am ill-prepared
For perils I need to face,
One tiny oar to beat the waves,
No rhythm, no well-planned pace.
I pass the boats who are heading to sea,
They wave and wish me well.
They look like they're going to Heaven
While I feel like I'm going to Hell.
Sometimes I dare to put down my oar
To see how far I have come.
I am no closer to where I am going
And just barely past where I am from.
My boat is filling with water,
I fear that it will sink.
Between bailing out water and fighting the tide,
There's no time for me to think.
When all my strength has left me,
I lie down and hope to die.
"You failed again," my mind does say,
"So why do you even try?"
I think of the boats who passed me
That looked so wise and so serene.
They seemed to know where they were going
While I hardly know where I've been.
I came to this earth to learn to be me.
If I don't accept me, who will?
I fight the tide because that's who I am
And when I'm dying, I'll be fighting it still.

To understand that there really is a process of life, one only has to take a look at Nature. Look at the sensibility of the seasons, the way birds and leaves disappear in the fall and return in the spring. Look at the total genius that goes into creating the human body as it grows in the mother's womb. There is a process that takes place in relationships, and only upon looking back at them do we see the route taken to get to the present state. In 2002, as mentioned earlier, my husband and I celebrated our 25th anniversary and we hosted a huge gala event. To some people the party would have been the gift, but although it was the best celebration of my whole life, the greatest gift was having the opportunity to look back to see where we had been. I had decided that if we were not honestly joyful at having made it this far, then we would not be hypocritical enough to throw a party to commemorate our "success." I looked back and saw the hard work, the struggles, and the near misses, and I knew without a doubt that we had been part of a process that made perfect sense in hindsight.

I truly believe that we are all part of a master plan in which no person is more important than any other no matter the physical trappings that may surround them. Some people who have riches and fame often have a false sense of grandiosity and self-importance that appears tiny in the larger scheme of things. I believe that a homeless person or derelict drunk on the street has just as much greatness as the leader of a country, a top-notch athlete, or a philanthropist who devotes his or her life to the betterment of society. They just have different roles to play; in this feature presentation called Life, there are no starring roles.

In fact, the derelict has agreed to play a role in direct opposition to the person whose success in life is measured by the status or the riches that person has acquired. How would we measure the so-called success of the CEO of a Fortune 500 company, or the leader of a country, if we did not know that homeless people exist? If every person on earth were a leader, there would be no need of leaders because there would be no followers. If there were no criminals, then there would be no law-abiding citizens. There is a definite process in the hierarchy of human existence. If there was no "here" then there would be no "there." We only exist because of our differences and opposites. Thank God for the differences. (For more detailed explanations on this topic, read *Conversations With God* by Neale Donald Walsch.)

As mentioned in the last paragraph of Chapter 21, I have learned that *when I feel the most out of control, that is when I am getting the most help.* I am consciously unaware of the activity in the background of my life, so there have been times when I have assumed that nothing is going on and that I am all alone; I become very scared, because at that time, I do not have a clue how to handle all of my problems. In despair, I may cry out for help, and I always get it.

There have been times in my life when I thought that I had all the answers and was totally in charge. One of those times occurred in 1999 when Sean needed my help. He had created a program called Peace Theatre and had to find a way to implement it. He had created a way to use drama to bring about resolution to conflicts between any numbers or groups of people. *CAUSE Canada* asked him if he would like to test it out on the former child soldiers at a mission in Sierra Leone, West Africa. He agreed to do it, but he had to come up with the money to pay his own airplane fare. I wrote and sent out a fund-raising letter to 500 people and 16% of those asked sent in contributions. Within two months he had enough money to go but I felt like a failure because so few had contributed. Sean later told me that 16% is phenomenal and that a successful campaign is one that gets 6% positive feedback.

I found myself making judgments about *who would give, who should give, who would not give.* Sometimes I was right, but mostly I was surprised. I learned many valuable lessons while doing that project. One of the most important was that "You can ask, but sometimes the answer is NO!" and conversely "If you don't ask, you won't know if the answer would have been YES!" For some reason, I zeroed in on one woman who had been in that seminar I mentioned earlier and decided that she would surely contribute $20 to the cause. When, after two months, my son had not heard from her, I chose to be hurt. We met at a seminar reunion in July (about three months after the letter went out) and she came straight over to see me. She handed me a very heavy container in the shape of a miniature milk can.

She apologized for it being so late, but went on to explain that she teaches drama to junior high students. When she got my letter she read it to her class, and they were so impressed that Sean was using drama to bring about peace that they unanimously agreed to donate all of the proceeds from their annual "end of the year" play to his cause. That explained why it was so late—the play did not take place until the end of June. There was $429.38 in the can, which turned out to be one of the biggest donations that Sean received. This was a huge lesson for me because I had wanted her donation to be given according to my schedule; if she had done that, Sean would have only received $20. With the Universe being in charge of the process, he gratefully received 2100% more. Work was being done in the background by higher forces and I should have *trusted the process.*

I have one more story that illustrates that we are being

taken care of, that we will get what we need when we need it. In 1990, I was still struggling to get past my depression days; sometimes I succeeded but sometimes I did not. I felt quite useless most of the time and scored zero in the confidence department. I was feeling like a failure because I had not been able to handle university. Because I did not know where to else to go, I took a job in a retail store in one of the malls in Edmonton.

I was all by myself in the store one night when a woman came up to me with a huge excited grin on her face. As she came up to me she shrieked, "Oh my God! Is that really you?" I was so embarrassed for her. I stammered, "I'm sorry, but I don't know you. You must be mistaking me for someone else." She apologized and sheepishly went on looking for whatever she had come in for. I know people get mistaken for other people all the time, but this is where the interesting part comes in. The woman came back to me and said, "I just have to tell you. You are the spitting image of my friend, Laurene Patterson. It's amazing!" For a moment, I could not speak. *I knew Laurene Patterson!* The woman had no further interest in me even though I told her, even more amazingly, that I knew the person she had mistaken me for. She just walked out of the store, leaving me standing there feeling dumbstruck. You wonder why!

When I was in training to be a lab technician at the University Hospital in Edmonton, Laurene Patterson was assigned to teach me how to take blood from patients. I absolutely adored this woman. She was pretty to look at and fun to be around. She had lovely red hair and always had a smile on her face. I remember thinking that if I had my choice to be any other person on earth, it would be Laurene. Well, it would seem that I got my wish because that day I was told by a perfect stranger that I looked exactly like her. When I went home that night, still shaken by the night's events, I walked up the stairs to my bedroom. As I turned on the light and looked in mirror, for one second I saw Laurene. If I could be mistaken for a person that I had idolized, I can't be all bad! That night I decided that God was telling me that I *am* pretty, I *am* special, and I *am* a nice person—when I thought I was none of those things. He heard my wish 20 years earlier and saved it for a day when I would need it. So you see there really is a process going on that is completely out of our hands and I am so glad that there is. That night, my self-image took a real turn for the good; my faith in the Universe went up a notch or two as well.

The easiest thing to do is to trust the process when everything is going well or easy in your life—when you are in a section of the river where the sailing is smooth. The hardest thing to do is to trust that same process when you are bashing against the rocks and the wind is carrying you from one side of the river to the other; when the weather is changing from bad to worse. When you are feeling that much out of control, all you have to do is to hand the control over to God (whoever that may be to you) and trust that you will be taken care of. I have all this firsthand information and all this amazing faith, but still I experience days when I wonder how I will make it to the next part of my journey—how will I make it over that next pile of rocks that I did not expect because it was just under the surface of the water?

On those days, when I feel most alone, I have to reach way down inside and grasp on to the part of me that knows one day of the journey is just as important as the next. There are stretches of the river where there is little action going on. Some call them smooth sailing sections while others see them as *boring*. Every solitary drop of water is necessary to create the total river that is my life. Every inch of distance traveled is one inch closer to the destination—the almighty ocean. There are times when action is necessary (when you have to swim like crazy) and there are times when it is appropriate to just tread water. I am learning to trust that I will know what to do when I find myself wondering how to handle some particular part of the trip.

CHAPTER 24

The next thing that I had to do to stay on the road to health was to face my fears—not just talk about them, but turn around and look them square in the eye. I explained much earlier that my mother, leaving to go to my grandmother's funeral, taught me to fear abandonment and to be afraid of showing any negative feelings. My mother punishing me for going to the coal yard taught me to be afraid of humiliation of any kind, to be afraid of authority figures, to be afraid of getting dirty, to be afraid to be friends with boys, and to be afraid of being spontaneous. My father going away to Europe after the war taught me to fear that men I love will probably sneak out in the night and leave me; he taught me that I must do everything possible to keep him, and any future men in my life, smiling and happy, no matter the cost to me. Fear became the only thing I trusted because I always knew exactly where to find it, and I knew that it would never let me down.

It only took me 55 years to discover that I do not dislike fear; *I thrive on it.* I feel comfortable when I am afraid. For many years fear was the only emotion I would admit to; it was safe. As long as I was afraid, I knew I was alive. Not long ago, I told our daughter Lindsey that I was "scared spitless" (not my exact words!) about a speech I was scheduled to give. She said, "That's when you do your best work—you thrive on fear!" I knew she was right and I had a good laugh because I was not as far out of the woods as I thought; I sure did not think that anyone else had noticed. By the way, I gave a great speech!

I honestly thought that I kept my fear so hidden that no one else could see it. Lindsey had surprised me, but she was not the first person to see right through me. When I was a participant in the seminar in 1999, we had to stand up and say, exactly and truthfully, what our first impression was of each other person in the room. The facilitator said to me, "I see so much fear in you that you are almost catatonic." I started to cry. The others thought that I was hurt by her honest—and accurate—comment, but really I was relieved that my secret was out and in front of all those people!

When I first started public speaking in 2002, I discovered a very important and useful thing about fear. I thought about the way I feel when I am afraid to do something that is just a part of everyday life—something that I have a choice in how I feel about it—for instance, public speaking, writing exams, or starting a new job. I am not talking about death-defying heart-stopping fearful situations. When I feel afraid to give a speech:

I feel nauseated.

My hands get clammy.

I feel sweaty all over.

My heart beats like a runaway locomotive.

I have trouble concentrating.

I feel like I have to pee.

Then I thought about how I feel when I am really excited:

I feel nauseated.

My hands get clammy.

I feel sweaty all over.

My heart beats like a runaway locomotive.

I have trouble concentrating.

I feel like I have to pee.

So . . . if fear and excitement both feel the same, then *why not choose to be excited?*

Use this as a test. Which sounds better as an introductory line in a speech?

I am so scared to be up here in front of you this evening! OR *I am so excited to be up here in front of you this evening!*

Fear is caused by pain. The best way to know if you are afraid (even though it looks like anger, frustration, sadness, jealousy, guilt, or hatred) is to ask yourself, "Am I behaving with love?" If the answer is no, then you are acting out of fear. There are only two major emotions—*fear* and *love.* So when I feel angry, I now ask myself, "Marilyn, what are you afraid of?" As soon as I ask, the anger starts to dissipate as though its secret is out: "Phew! She doesn't need me anymore; she's figured out that she's not irate, she's afraid." The next step is to identify the fear, which is not necessarily an overwhelming task—it just takes brutal honesty! And the interesting thing is that as soon as I ask the question, I calm down enough to at least promise myself that I am going to work on finding out what the answer is.

Sometimes I feel like fear is coming at me from all angles. I can turn around and around, trying desperately to literally keep the fear at arm's length, but the only two solid surfaces that I have to use as blocks are the palms of my hands. That is just not good enough. So one day in sheer frustration I stood still, put my arms out, and I gathered the fear around me, pulling it to my body the same way I would hug a small child. I stood for quite a while holding my arms as though I was hugging myself. Within minutes, I could feel the fear and the pain slipping away. I opened up my arms and all that was there was air, no fear at all. I realized I had created that fear; I owned that fear, so only I could make that fear disappear. I literally embraced my fear and felt wonderful. I felt free and peaceful. I could not believe the power that was mine at that moment. I still do this whenever I feel overwhelmed by something, even if it is stemming from something concrete. No matter the cause; the fear is of my creation and only I can dispel it. That, my friend, is one more example of sheer magic!

Fear is like a cat; the more you call for it, the more it runs away. Stand still for a minute and appear uninterested, and the cat will be right there rubbing up against you. Fear behaves in exactly the same way. In the early 1980s, I was treated for agoraphobia, which according to the Greek translation means "fear of the marketplace." Today it is interpreted as "fear of open spaces" or "fear of leaving your home." The main symptom of a phobia is panic attacks, which can feel quite life-threatening. The therapist taught us that to avoid a panic attack, ask for it to happen. When you want one to start, it is impossible to make it happen. Fear is a spineless creature; it only attacks those who are afraid of it, those who are paralyzed by it. Fear is one guest who only arrives when it is not invited! Once I learned that I was creating the fear, I was able to start defeating that wretched condition.

I have heard people say that they do not want to go into

therapy because they are too afraid to face or feel the pain that they know will arise when they let their minds go back to their childhoods. This always amazes me, but that is probably because I did face and feel my childhood pain, and I came out feeling wonderful. The victory I felt in my soul was indescribable and, truthfully, it really was better than sex! Think about it. We, as children, can live in the pain and survive, but we adults cringe and say that we cannot go there. It is like sending your son or daughter to the dentist when you are too terrified to do the same. Only when I was willing to go back and remember the pain, feel the pain, and embrace the pain did the pain start to go away. I had to acknowledge that it was in me before I could send it anywhere else.

We all have a past that truly does affect the present and can certainly predict the future if it is left unacknowledged. Recently someone close to me said, "The past should be left in the past," after a memory had surfaced that made him experience a great deal of pain. I told him that I disagreed and pointed out that if he would choose to deal with it, he would not feel such agony at just the remembrance of it.

I believe that you can deny your past, dwell in your past, or deal with your past. I chose to deal with it. The victory I felt in doing so was far greater than the pain had ever been. I was actually quite amazed how mild the pain was once I was *willing to feel it*. I think I know why. The pain was created by a child, and children always magnify everything they do. They cry with gusto when they merely scrape a knee or when they are denied their favorite treat. I am not saying their pain was just imagined; I am saying that what was excruciating to the child will be much more tolerable to the adult. Yes, it will still hurt, but not as imagined.

(I will concede that the older you are when the painful

event happens, the longer it will take to effectively deal with it. That is because the older you are, the higher your tolerance will be and thus the more pain it will take to actually scar you.)

I also found a couple of tricks for dealing with pain, fear, or worries—like most inventions they were created out of desperation. I was tired of lying in bed at night worrying about money, about whether or not my husband loved me, about the weather, about any other irrational thing that came into my head. I got weary of the effort it took to keep going over and over the same fears and concerns night after night.

One night I decided that I could not take all the wild thinking anymore, so I created something positive to get rid of all that negativity. I imagined a field on the other side of the world, beside which live many thousands of poverty-stricken people. The field had long ago been depleted of nutrients and unable to grow anything for many years. I decided to imagine planting one flower in that field for every worry or negative thought that came into my head. I created hundreds of flowers of all different varieties; the bigger my problem, the more beautiful and healthier the flower would be. In my mind, I literally turned negative energy into beautiful positive energy that would cheer up all those hungry people. I tried to imagine the awe that they would feel when they saw this barren piece of land bursting into bloom. (I probably could have chosen to grow something these starving people could eat, but decided that sometimes food for the soul is just as welcome and just as nourishing.) I found that as soon as I changed a thought into a flower, it disappeared from my mind. I replanted flowers in that field many times over until one day I did not need to plant anymore. Negative turned to positive; bad turned to good; fear turned to love; and ugliness turned into something beautiful.

One day I was beside myself with confusion and mental

overload. I was concerned about each of the kids for different reasons; I was concerned about money; I was concerned about anything and everything—real or imagined. I was going in circles just trying to keep all the problems straight so that I could worry about each and every one of them in turn with equal amounts of anguish. Finally, I thought that I was going to explode and that is how I came up with this task for myself.

I wrote all the problems on little pieces of paper, then put on my coat and headed off to the park. Without looking at what was written on each paper, I dug holes under trees and buried my problems in them. As I put each into the ground, I said, "Now stay there and out of my mind until I dig you up." There were so many trees in that park that I never would remember where I buried them, but it did not matter because I went home with a clear head. I did not worry about them again. Within a few days, I had a hard time remembering what the problems were—there was no memory left of them.

So whatever happened to Lulubelle? I believe she was with me until I realized she should not be. In my earlier years, I never thought about her because she had been there for so long and I assumed everyone had someone just like her. She served me well, and kept the fun side of me alive until I could handle it on my own. I hated her and I loved her. I honored Lulubelle in this poem so that you could see exactly what happened to the two of us in the end.

WHOLE IS A SUM OF THE PARTS

Lulubelle with the laughing eyes,
So full of mischief and playful at heart.
A part of me I left in my past, but now, integration must start.
Her love she gave without question,
So easy, she was used in return.
She dared to balance her life on the edge,
And joke about Hell where she'd burn.
Lulubelle had another side,
She brought smiles when someone was down.
Many times, she entertained for hours on end,
Her name reflects how she felt like a clown.
Lulubelle didn't know the meaning of fear,
No need-I had both of our shares.
I cried, she laughed; I sighed, she sang,
Her whole world seemed devoid of all cares.
The battle surged on between us, but her presence let me survive.
I hated the fact that he loved her!
Did he even know that I was alive?
Her fun, my guilt; her laughter, my tears
Became more than I could endure.
I went inside to a place that was mine-
Her death was my self-prescribed cure!
But how can I kill a part of myself
That's as real as my hand or my face?
I tried to stifle her laughter; her beauty I tried to erase.
For many years I have lived my life,
The girl behind the closed door.
There has been a void within me, where Lulubelle lived before.

Not she, who made him happy; nor she, with talents galore!
It was me, who gave her power and charm,
It was me, who gave gifts and more!
Now Lulubelle stands before me,
I walk slowly-my hand, I extend.
She smiles as she sees my welcome,
I embrace her, my oldest friend!
Now we are one-the whole is me, and together we'll face any foe.
I now feel free to be happy!
I now have the power to grow!

Something that may have helped her to leave my life was that I changed my name. As I mentioned in the Preface, I had always hated the name Judy. Even as I say it and write it now, I think it sounds ridiculous and I apologize to any other women named Judy who are reading this book. I only had a problem with *my* Judy. However, after writing this book, I feel a kindness towards that name, because the little girl who had it was so very sweet and so very brave. It is a fact that when I say it, my mouth turns down; whereas "Marilyn" makes my face muscles turn up, as though in a smile. I know that *my* Judy had a hard time within herself and so, in dropping her from my name, I felt like I was giving her a well-earned rest. I often think of her and when I do, I see her smiling within me. I know she feels happy now that she is away from all that hard work that is required to be a human being.

Amazingly, my life changed when my name changed. My family and friends expect more of Marilyn than they did of Judy. Marilyn learned to swim; Judy was terrified of water. Marilyn loves public speaking while Judy felt better staying in the background. (Remember she wanted to work in windowless basements!) Marilyn is stronger and more able to stand on her own; Judy needed Lulubelle. In all, Marilyn is happier than Judy ever was. When I was Judy, my husband used to call me all sorts of sweet names such as *darling, sweetie, honey, princess*, and so on. I loved him calling me those affectionate pseudonyms, but when I changed my name, he immediately started calling me Marilyn most of the time. After a while I asked him why he was calling me Marilyn when he had never called me Judy. He replied, "Because you *are* Marilyn—you never *were* Judy." Other people had some trouble with the change at first, but not for long. They eventually all said that my new name suited me better than Judy ever had. When I first changed it, Mom asked me why and I replied, "You gave me two names, Judith and Marilyn, so I thought you meant for me to use Judy for one half of my life and Marilyn for the other!" She thought that was funny.

CHAPTER 25

I have talked about the things that happened in the years prior to my breakdown, in the years when I felt like I was in the bottomless pit, and in the years following my illness. I have talked about some of the concepts that helped me to grow and heal; I feel so blessed that the knowledge of them came into my reality. I have told you about the incident on the clothesline when I was a child, and how my mother, by her action that day, did much to negatively change the way I thought about myself. I cannot leave this story without talking about my mother's life and how we interacted through most of our years together. I would not be in my present state of health if I had not taken the opportunity to delve into our often troubled relationship. Because I did not set out consciously to heal my relationship with Mom, I am very grateful that I was willing to listen and take notice of the opportunities that the Universe gave to us to do it anyway. I hope by telling this part of my story that you will see how working on a relationship can have wonderful results that truly do last for the rest of one's lifetime. This is a brief look at my mother's story.

My mother grew up in extreme poverty, dirt, chaos, and in the company of many forms of abuse. My grandparents separated after it was discovered that my grandfather had been abusing my mother's half-sister, his stepdaughter. My grandmother, now running her own farm, was a hard-working, honest woman who was so busy working in the fields with the men that she had no time for housework and motherly chores. Mom often went to school wearing dirty clothes and was teased by the other children because of it. When she was 9 years old Mom was sent lovingly and sadly to live at her grandmother's as a way of giving her a more stable household to grow up in. Her mother loved her enough to do what was best for her, but even though the intent was good, I have often wondered what interpretation Mom, as a child, took from the fact that she was sent away. As an adult Mom always said, "Mother sent me away because she loved me and because she felt that I would have a better life away from the chaos."

She also grew up in the hardships of the Great Depression and she has many stories about the extreme food shortage and how many days there was nothing to eat except potatoes. She had a hard life and I doubt that I have heard even a fraction of what it really was like. Mom is a loyal daughter and sister, and has complained little about her life as a child. I believe that from her, I learned that no matter how bad it is, you remain loyal to family. She also showed me that one should keep secrets from the rest of the world to protect one's family; as you can see, I did not follow her example on that point.

By going to live with her grandmother who lived a quiet and orderly life, in comparison to her parents, Mom learned many skills that she would not have gained had she not gone there. She learned to bake, cook, and sew to perfection. Her grandmother was a stern but fair taskmaster and because of that Mom developed an unbelievable work ethic before she ever stepped out into the world. Because of my great-grandmother's teachings, Mom was successful as a housekeeper to wealthy families and amazing as chief cook and pastry maker for two summers at the Paris Tea Room in Banff, Alberta.

By the time she met and married my father in 1938, she was an accomplished cook, baker, seamstress, knitter, and house-keeper. Dad got a very good deal when he married this woman who he had met only two months earlier. My sister, Sharon, was born in 1940 and my sister, Barbara, in 1942. In 1947, while on holidays with Dad and my sisters, Mom took ill and, thinking she was dying, went to the doctor only to be told that she was pregnant—not sick. Apparently, my birth had not been in the plans and Mom was quite distraught over the news. She made the statement that if she had to have another child, "let it be a boy." I guess God had other plans for her and the girl who would be me! Mom got her wish for a boy in 1953, when David was born.

Apparently Mom was not the same personality after my birth as she was before. She told me that she experienced depression after I came along, while she had not done so after my sisters' births. My sister Barbara said that Mom changed overnight when I was born. Apparently Mom used to play with my sisters a lot, taking them to the playground and so on, but she never did that with me—not once. Mom did not play with my sisters anymore after my birth either.

My memories of my mom for the rest of my growing-up years were as follows: Mom was an extremely hard-working housewife—I think of her as a "workaholic housewife." She was a superwoman in the house:

She baked all our bread, buns, pastries, cakes, and cookies.

She cooked fabulous meals even when food was in short supply.

She grew a big garden and canned all the vegetables and fruits for winter.

She knitted all our sweaters, hats, mitts, scarves, and occasionally our socks.

She sewed most of our clothes.

She was a good carpenter—she built shelves and other things as needed.

She painstakingly dug out our basement when it flooded.

She did all the other household chores like laundry and housecleaning.

She helped her uncle build a bedroom for my sisters and me.

She did all kinds of needlepoint and painted many pictures that decorated our walls then and many other people's walls now—especially mine.

Mom gave us the best life that she could; in retrospect, I know that she was on a mission to wipe out all the negatives of her growing-up years and, for the most part, she succeeded. The only thing wrong with this scene is that a mother who does that much work has no time for little girls.

When I think of Mom when I was a little girl, I hear clanging pots and pans; the monotonous sound of the washing machine; the kneading of bread; the click of knitting needles; the whirring of the flour sifter; the clickety-clack of the sewing machine treadle; the plop of cookie dough hitting the sides of the mixing bowl; the growl of the vacuum cleaner and the swish of a mop on the floor. Once in a very long while, I would even hear Mom singing, but not very often. I remember sitting in the living room playing "library," wishing with all my heart that for just a minute, my mother—my very hard-working mother—would come into the living room and talk to me. One afternoon when I was 4 years old I got my wish and we had a tea party that was special enough to remember 55 years later.

For my sake, if not for anyone else's, I need to reiterate that I loved my mother very much. My only wish in life was to have some positive attention from her. It is hard to fault a mother who worked so hard and who took no time for herself in her pursuit of creating a good and clean home for us. I cannot fault her on the physical life that she created for us; she just worked so hard, doing so much, that she had little left for us emotionally.

My father and I were extremely close and at times I could almost feel an ownership of him because he gave me more time than he gave to any of the others. I think I deserved it because I worked very hard to keep him happy and smiling. Dad adored my mother; I do not remember a day that he did not tell her that he loved her. However, in spite of his adoration, he rarely got up from his chair to help her. She kept his house in spotless condition, served him wonderful food, and kept the finances in order. I do not remember him doing much of anything to help—maybe that was the way it was back then, before women got the equality that was supposed to get them "out of the kitchen." The only thing I remember Dad doing was mowing the lawn. With Mom not being available, I really clung to my Dad. When he was home I felt safe and I felt loved. When he was gone, I just waited for his return. I have done a lot of waiting for men in my lifetime.

I know I touched on this a bit about my dad, but if anyone were to ask me what was missing from my growing-up years, it would be that neither of my parents ever told me of my gifts, my talents, my strong points, or even my weaknesses. I knew that they liked good grades, because when I got them, I got their high praise and I loved it. However, if something seemed scary, I would not do it because I had not been shown how to handle anything fearful; I did not have the knowledge inside that told me that dreams really do come true—so dream big! No one ever told me that I was invincible, until I met John, my husband. By then, however, the fear was firmly implanted. I begrudge the fact that I have many talents and for most of my life did not get any encouragement even when I asked for it. Whenever I tried something new, I always reverted to child-hood thinking and yearned for my mother's approval. I may have gotten it, but it did not look the way I wanted it to, and it was never given to me unless I asked. That only changed in the last few years of Mom's life.

Another thing that was a gift in reverse is that my parents never fought or argued in front of us. We do not even know if they did when they were away from us. This was a good thing in some ways except that it made me fearful of fighting with anyone—I did not know there was such a thing as constructive arguments. By not arguing even once in a while, I surmised that something bad must be going to happen if they did. This cursed me for a long, long time. Only in the last ten years have I been able to have a heated argument with John without cry-ing in panic. He laughs at me now remembering how I used to literally cringe when I thought we were going to have a dis-agreement. I think sometimes he wishes that I would go back to that because now I do not let us stop until we are totally sorted.

I grew up, got married to Dan, and left home. I think that my most harmonious time with my mom was during my young married years. She was great to us and she was a lovely grand-ma to my precious boys. After my split up with Dan, my moth-er was right there for me and did much to help me set up my new home with my sons. I cannot fault her for anything during those years. She did not ask any questions about my breakup with Dan because I asked her not to. She babysat for me when I needed it. She even picked up the boys in British Columbia after one of their annual summer visits with their father and drove them home for me. She was a good mom and a wonderful grandmother.

I especially admired her when dad was dying. My brother Dave and I arrived in Ladysmith to see Dad one more time and we expected to see Mom in a shambles. Instead, when she opened the door to let us in, she was a picture in light. I had steeled myself to be there to hold her up in her pain, but when I saw her strength shining through, my knees collapsed and I almost fell down on her doorstep. The whole time we were there, she took care of me as though as I was a fragile child once more. I could see the angels at work with her and she was a marvel until after Dad died five weeks later.

When Mom was widowed we had a lot of time to get to know one another out of the shadow of my father. She was great fun and spent a lot of time at our house out at Cooking Lake. I have many happy memories of her at that time: the day she fell up to her elbows in fresh cement in our driveway, laughing so hard that she almost fell in a second time headfirst; leg wrestling with the boys on the family room floor; driving to my house at 7 am to wait for my new furniture to arrive while I went to work; letting me pluck her eyebrows and doing such a thorough job that when I was done, she had none left. Luckily for me, Mom thought that was hilarious!

When I was about 40, Mom and I found ourselves arguing about most anything that came between us. Some said that we were too much alike, but I did not see that at all; furthermore, I did not *want* to see it. Sometimes I just felt like I was a horrible person, so what else could we expect? It got so bad for a few years that John did not like even being in the same room with us. Mom and I loved each other, but something was wrong between us. When John and I went to Arizona for two months in 1998, Mom was very upset because, even though we fought a lot, I was the one who was with her the most, so we invited her to come see us there for two weeks. During the first six weeks that we were away I was very homesick and the only thing that helped was to phone Mom because she *always* made me feel better. Then when she came for the visit, we fought about everything. It was craziness.

Over the years, John and I gave Mom some beautiful and plentiful gifts for all the various special occasions. I would be all excited about what we had chosen for her, but when she opened the gift she would barely even crack a smile over it. Sometimes I would say, "OK, Mom, this is the time to be excited. Now give us a big smile!" On those occasions she would laugh (we all loved it when Mom laughed!), the ice would break, and she would be happy about the gift. There were a few exceptions, like the time I gave her a doll to keep her company. I have a picture of her just smiling and hugging it to bits. I wondered if she had ever had a doll before. Other times, she would thank us much later, or I would hear her tell a friend that "John and Marilyn gave me the nicest gift . . . ," then continue to tell that person all about it. Or I would hear later from one of her friends how much she had loved something that we had given her but about which she had made little comment to us. On one birthday, we gave Mom an entertainment center. While John was putting it together, we kept waiting for her to say that she liked it. She said not a word, but then months later she said that it was just the best thing. I shook my head in puzzlement.

One day after her telling me some more stories about her

childhood, I realized that there was a very good and likely reason why Mom never got as excited about gifts as I would have liked her to. One Christmas, when she was a very young child, she received one gift—a coloring book. She was so happy about it because her family was too poor to have such things around. She adored that book. Then one day, her cousin Dorothy stole her treasured book, and she never saw it again. She got a gift; she loved her gift; and she lost her gift. From then on, I think that she refused to get excited about anything she received until she really knew it was hers for keeps. That was one of *her* childhood survival rules, I guess.

Another time, when I was writing our family history book, I asked my sisters and brother to each write a three-page story about their lives. After I had finished editing and typing them all up, Mom asked if she could read them. I handed her a copy of each child's story, including my own. I sat there as she read them, and I could hardly wait until she got to mine. I so wanted her to tell me that it was wonderful and that I was such a good writer. She had something nice to say about Sharon's; she had some praise about Barbara's; and she said how she loved that David was so funny. I waited with baited breath for her glowing comments about mine. Mom read it and then simply said, "Well, you certainly are wordy, aren't you!" I felt like she had kicked me in the stomach.

When I got my breath back I started to cry and told Mom that she had no idea how much she had hurt me. I told her that I was the writer in the family, and I was the one putting together our whole darned family history, and I was the only one she did not give a compliment to. She told me that she just expects me to do well because I have always succeeded at everything that I have put my mind to doing. We both cried— somehow she and I always found a way to hurt one another.

In 2002, as mentioned earlier, John and I celebrated our 25th wedding anniversary with a huge party and Mom was very excited about it. She said that it felt like she was going to our wedding because in 1977 she had been unable to attend because my dad was dying. Before our party, Mom and I went shopping for a new dress for her to wear. She said that she wanted to make me proud of her, so she wanted to look her best. We picked out a great dress and I was proud of her. She looked so sweet and so fragile—best of all, she was my mom and she was there.

It was a wonderful party, so I was surprised a couple of days later when Mom said something about it that really hurt my feelings. She said it was a nice party but if she had to listen to one more nice thing being said about us, she thought she was going to puke. We were on the phone when she said it, so as soon as I could speak, I told her that I was going to hang up and I did. I did not care at the time if I ever spoke to her again.

On about the seventh day of silence, I got a call from "Life Line." Mom wore one of their buzzers around her neck like a necklace and she was to push the button if she was hurt or sick. Apparently her buzzer had sounded but when the emergency operator called her to make sure it was not a false alarm, Mom did not answer. As I was a contact person, I was asked what I wanted them to do. I told the man to call an ambulance because I could not get there fast enough to check on her myself. He said he would, and he would also call the manager in charge of the seniors' complex where she lived and tell her to look for Mom. The caller said someone would call me back.

I hung up the phone and stood there. I happened to glance at the calendar and saw something that I had not realized until that very minute; it was the anniversary of my father's death. I thought how ironic it would be if Mom died that day, too, while I was still mad at her. Suddenly I felt a bubble of peace form around me and I remember praying aloud, saying, "Dear God, if this is the day that my mom is to die, then so be it. I will have to live with the guilt of being angry at her. However, if there is any way that you can let her live at least one more day, then I promise that I will go and clear up this pain between us." At that very moment the phone rang and it was Mom. She was mad and embarrassed because she came out of the laundry room only to see ambulance attendants coming down the hall to get her. She insisted that she did not push the button, so no one knows what happened. The design of the buzzer was such that it was hard to push it unintentionally. I truly believe it was just meant to be a wake-up call for me.

True to my promise to God, I told Mom that I would be coming over to see her the next day. I was nervous about confronting her, but as I got closer to her apartment I felt the warm comfort of strength coming over me; it had nothing to do with anger, but everything to do with love and empowerment. When I got to Mom's place, we immediately sat down. I told her how much she had hurt me. She said that she had been joking about the party, but I said that it was just the last of many roadblocks that were keeping us apart, and we needed to talk. I said *everything* that was on my mind and I was surprised how it all just flowed out of me; she sat there listening very intently and, unbelievably, she did not shed a tear. She just listened and I know that she heard me. We talked for a long time; afterwards, we both felt amazingly better.

A month earlier, in February 2002, I was asked to give two talks (one of them being the story about my stepson Andrew's life) to a group of addicts at a halfway house. The other talk was called "I'm a Survivor" and it involved the story about Mom hanging me on the clothesline. That was one of the family secrets so, in telling it, I felt like a traitor. I knew that I was making Mom the villain in the story, but I did not realize how successful I was until one of the men at the session asked me, very seriously, if I wanted him to arrange with a guy to "off her." I just about croaked and told him, "Of course not!" It was all right for me to be mad at my mother, but no one else better be!

In my guilt, I went to Mom and told her about the talk that I had given and planned to give again. She told me that she would give me her blessing to use the story on one condition: every time I tell the story, she asked me to say that she did what she did because she loved me and was trying to protect me from the dangers of the coal mine. I agreed to that and did as she asked. Happily, my story (as well as Andrew's) helped many men at the center.

In the summer of 2002, right in the middle of the busiest year of my life, Mom began to have some problems living on her own. She has stopped cooking for herself and was basically not eating at all. Of course, we were all very worried about her, so John and I arranged for her to move from her apartment to a more care-oriented seniors' facility. There she would get a little more attention and she had to eat her meals in the dining room with the other elderly residents. If she failed to show up for a meal, a nurse would be sent to check on her.

So at the end of July, I took two weeks off and helped Mom pack and move. At the beginning when I realized that I was the only one available to help her, I took on the martyr role and played it to the hilt. I cried the blues and whined and moaned like you would not believe. I should have been shot! Anyway, one day, with my martyr's badge firmly in place, Mom and I began the awesome task of breaking down her life into "only what could be held in one small bedroom."

We all take our possessions for granted and assume they are ours for life. We do not think about the day when we will have to downsize and get rid of anything not absolutely essential. We lined up a bunch of boxes, each one having the name of a loved one or the words *garbage* or *church bazaar* on it. It floored me how hard our task was going to be. And so we made our first stab at my mother's world.

The first thing Mom pulled out of a drawer was a black and white framed photo of Mount Rundle in Banff. As a premonition of what this task was going to be like, Mom started to cry her heart out, then told me that it was the first gift that my father had ever given her in 1939. My heart stopped. How could she start giving such things away? Needless to say, I offered, with gratitude, to take that picture and guard it with my life; it is now hanging here on the wall right beside me as I am writing this.

Sometimes the sorting was tedious, but most of the time it was just plain heartbreaking. My memories of the move involve a lot of scenes of the two of us sitting on the floor with some object in our hands about which we are talking, laughing, or crying—or a little bit of each. Mom would tell me anything that came to mind about each item; I swear that I learned more about her life in those two weeks than I ever knew before. Sometimes she would see me crying all alone over an item that brought back memories. She would sit down with me and we would hold each other. Other times, we would sit in silence, just looking at something, then Mom would sigh as she made her decision as to which box to put it into. It was long, hard work and it was the most precious thing that I have ever done in my whole life.

When I was working in the kitchen I pulled out Mom's boxes of recipe cards and cookbooks. I asked her what she wanted me to do with them and she said, "I don't care about any of them except my *Blue Ribbon Cookbook*—that's my Bible." I asked her why it was so special. She replied that she bought it in 1938 when she was working at the Paris Tea Room in Banff and that it had saved her life on many occasions when she needed instructions on how to cook something she had never done before. The pages were yellow and crisp and many of them had greasy fingerprints on them. I was in my snooty mood and could not think why anyone would want that, so I put it into the "indecisive box" that I would take home for sorting later.

That day I told Mom that because her apartment was so full of boxes she should come and sleep at our house until she moved into her new place. She said she would but she only lasted one night. That morning when I woke up, I could hear someone rummaging in the basement. My first thought was that the dogs were getting into Mom's boxes. I went down and saw my wee mother (she stood less that 5 feet tall and weighed about 80 pounds) searching through her things until she stood up victoriously, having found what she had been looking for. In one hand she had her favorite saucepan and in the other she had her bible, the *Blue Ribbon Cookbook*. She looked at me and said, "Take me home. I have my pot to make soup and I have my Bible in case anyone needs some cooking advice." By the determined look on her face, I knew it would be pointless to argue with her. We drove back to her apartment. I suspected that no matter how cluttered it was she was not going to give up her own space until she absolutely had to.

Later that day, John came to help us move some of the heavier boxes to make room for more. I was still working in the kitchen when John heard me crying. He asked me what was the matter *this time* and I held up a rusty old flour sifter and said, "This!" I told him how I remember the noise of it in the kitchen when I was little and that I could not imagine anyone else having it—so I took it! I cleaned off the rust and now it sits in my living room with silk flowers in it. I love it and every day when I see it, I remember my mom.

From that time on, we both felt differently about each other and it showed—so much of the animosity from both sides had dwindled to nothing. I learned that my mother, as was the case for many of the women of her generation, had put her whole self into the caring and nurturing of her family. One day, shortly after she moved, I arrived at Mom's room and found her crying; in her hands was her *Blue Ribbon Cookbook*. When I asked what was wrong, she said, "I am sad and I am lonely. I'm not needed anymore. Everyone I used to take care of is either dead or busy. Take this damned book—no one is going to need the advice of an old woman!" I took her cookbook home and it is now safe forever with some other treasures in a shadow box that I put together in honor of my parents. That, too, is on the wall here beside me. I look at it everyday and miss them both.

Mom, like many others, after working 24/7 for all her adult life, was retired without a bouquet of flowers, a gold watch, or a banquet; there was not even a pension to sweeten the deal. As I coupled her childhood with her dedication to us as an adult, I finally understood this amazing woman who I am proud to say was my mother.

A KIND AND GENTLE LADY

A kind and gentle lady
Has been in my life for so long.
So plagued by doubt and racked with pain,

For us, she tries to be strong.
The doubt is whether she deserves to be loved,
The pain-from ages past.
So long she has suffered she thinks it is she-
While still a child, her die had been cast.
She did everything a mother can do
To give her children what she never had.
From early dawn to darkest night
She slaved, but still she felt sad.
It merely was a common sight
To see this gentle lady cry.
Despair was spilling from out of her soul,
But nobody questioned why.
If I could have one wish in this life,
I would wish her one day of peace,
To let her feel the love that is hers,
I would wish that her pain would cease.
A word to this gentle lady from me,
"You didn't deserve the pain.
The little girl that was, still is-
just love her and she'll live again.
You think that you are too old to change,
when you're too old to change, you are dead.
If you embrace the child within you
she will make sense of the life you have led."
This kind and gentle lady
Who has been in my life all along
Gave me life and for that, I thank her,
From her I learned to be strong.

Marilyn Avient

In 2003 I launched my book of poems and gave a two-hour presentation about my life entitled "The Girl Behind the Closed Door," which is also the title of that book. I originally had asked my mom to stay offstage to listen because she cries so easily and I did not want to have to censor my words in order to avoid upsetting her. She pursed her lips and said in a no-nonsense kind of voice, "I will be sitting in the audience watching you and I will *not* cry!" And she was and she didn't!

Afterwards, she told me that she had been stuck to her seat like cement because she was so mesmerized by what I was saying. She told me that she had never known much of what I talked about, but that she understood me for, probably, the first time in my life. I explained that night in my speech why I had changed my name to Marilyn; previously, she always had trouble calling me that, but from then on she never mistakenly called me Judy again. The very next day, after my book launch, my sister Barbara phoned Mom and during their conversation, Barb called me Judy. She said that Mom told her in no uncertain terms, "Her name is Marilyn and I don't want you to ever call her Judy again."

Later that year, in a surprise development in our lives, I had to tell Mom that John and I were moving to Vancouver Island. Looking back, I cannot believe I did that; she depended on me so much, yet I had the nerve to leave her. She was happy for us on the outside, but I know on the inside she was devastated. She told me that it was my turn to have some fun and she was happy that I was going to be able to move to the island with John, just as she and Dad had done when she was exactly the same age as me. I loved her so much for that because, as much as I tried to deny it, I knew that I was breaking her heart. Of all the children, I had been her most constant caregiver, and I dared to leave.

The day I said good-bye to her was the closest that I have ever come to *absolutely* dissolving in tears. She said things to me that I would never have guessed were in her heart for me. All those things I had wanted all my life from my mom were, all of a sudden, mine. I will never forget her wee little body standing in that doorway trying to be strong for my sake. From that day on we never spoke another cross word to one another. I visited her as often as I could but, I know, it was not often enough. I wanted her to come and stay with us for as long as she liked, but she did not feel that she had the strength to make the trip.

After I thought I was finished writing this book, I found some files on my computer and in them was a letter, a very precious and important letter. It was a letter that I had written to Mom the day before we left for Vancouver Island. When I found it, I sobbed like there was no tomorrow; the pain of leaving her landed back on me with a thud. I closed the file, declaring that I would never read it again. However, as is often the case with me, I do not always have the last say in such things. You know how it is: *We plan; God laughs!*

The next day I went for a walk to try to calm down because I was feeling a little overwhelmed with all the exciting things that are happening to me with the publishing of this book. I asked Mom to please give me some help. I heard her say, *"Put in the letter."* I instantly calmed down and as soon as I got home, I did as she suggested. I am inserting the letter exactly as I found it—I do not want to change a word or even a punctuation mark. I want it to be left intact for always.

Sept 5, 2003

Dear Mom,

I haven't even left town yet and already I am writing this letter to you. I cannot believe that we are doing this thing—moving away from you and all else that is near and dear to us. However, I know that I am supposed to be doing this move and I also know that I am going to the one place in the world where I will feel more alive than anywhere else—Vancouver Island. I have fought the idea of living on an island all of my life. Just thinking about the fact that a very large body of water cuts me off from the rest of the country used to make me quiver in my boots and now it is one of the things that is luring me.

Have you ever done anything that you know is totally out of your range of possibilities and yet you are doing it and the closer you get to achieving the goal, the more at peace you feel with yourself? This is one of those situations and I know that God is very much behind this whole thing. I do not believe that I could be leaving you if I was not sure of that one fact. By knowing that the Universe is totally planning this for me, then I know that the same Universe will be taking care of you.

To think that for all those years I wasted time being angry at you for things you did not even know you had done. The child in me sought your approval and love for 54 years and only when I declared that I did not need it, did you give it to me beyond my wildest dreams. One day I will write and tell you all about that phase of my life, but for now I am just trying to deal with saying good-bye to you.

I could not have asked for a nicer day than we had yesterday together. We laughed and played cards and scrabble and except for the last hour I almost forgot that this was THE day that I had been dreading ever since that day when I was told that it was time for me to go to the island to live. I do not know how I got the courage to even spend such a day with you because the girl who was me in the past would have come over, said good-bye and left as quickly as possible. The moment I cherish the most was when we had hugged good-bye and you took my face in your hands and said, "Just let me have one more kiss from my little girl." Those words will go with me to my grave and I can finally say without one speck of doubt in my mind or in my soul that my mother loves me unconditionally and with her whole heart.

Mom, tomorrow we are driving away from this city that has been my home for most of my life and I am taking you with me in that piece of my heart that is yours and yours alone. For all my life you have heard me say that Dad was my favourite person on Earth, but you are the person who has had the deepest impact on me and I am so very proud to be your daughter. You are my heroine. You are my mom. May God, Dad, and the angels take care of you each and every day. Till we meet again, remember how much I love you,

Your littlest girl,

Marilyn

Mom died on March 13, 2005, and when I heard the news I completely fell apart in the shock of it. She was 86 years old, but still it was a shock. But, unlike after Dad's death, I picked myself up and handled everything the way that Mom would have wanted me to. I was honored and happy to give the eulogy at Mom's memorial service and I can honestly say that I had fun relating my favorite stories about her life. When Sharon, Barb, Dave, Pat, and I went through her room I found her copy of my book *The Girl Behind the Closed Door* in a drawer; inside was a letter to me that she knew would only be found after she was gone. She told me how proud she was of me and how I had exceeded her every dream for me. That was the topping on my cake; I had my mother's unconditional love and approval, and I finally felt complete, in spite of my loss.

And so you see, there is no relationship that cannot be healed and made whole, if the two people involved really have the wish to do so. Mom and I did not set out to do that, but the results of our "work" paid off and our last three years were the best of the lot. I would not be the happy woman I am today if we had not walked through that almost all-consuming fire together.

EPILOGUE

On September 8, 2003, we arrived at our new home on Vancouver Island still reeling from the trauma of saying good-bye to our beloved family and friends; I thought I would die of home-sickness for the first entire year. I missed the familiarity of my life in Edmonton and I missed the wonderful people who had been in it. The worst pain came from my constant worrying about my mom—I missed her tremendously. At first the novelty of the move was great; there was so much to do getting unpacked and settled in, but once that was done I could feel the old familiar black cloud settling over me once more. It got so bad that all my learnings from the past two decades had no effect on the sadness and loneliness into which I had let myself become so firmly enmeshed. John was doing a better job at making friends than I was; he joined a golf club and just naturally fell in with a group of nice men. He is one of those people that others are instantly drawn to.

After about six months I very tentatively told John that I needed to see a doctor because I was feeling so low. I thought he would get upset with me, but he lovingly said, "I think that would be a good idea." I guess he had noticed. So I went to my new family doctor who immediately referred me to the one and only psychiatrist in the area. She turned out to be the kind of doctor that my first doctor in Edmonton could have learned a lot from. For the second time in my life I was told that I was bipolar; the loss that I was experiencing, since leaving my life in Edmonton, had triggered a depression. She immediately started treating me with medications that made sense for me.

For all of 2002, the year before moving to the island, I had been on a "high" during which I went totally crazy with creativity. I could not stop. I was writing and speaking and creating and spending *lots* of money in the process. My concern, once I got balanced, was that I would never be truly happy again because the balanced me was really not much fun. I finally got it through my head that my talent was not dependent on my mood in order to exist. My talent was my talent and always would be—the manic phase (which always brought out my ultrahyped resourcefulness) was the sheer raw energy that gave me confidence to do my creating and that was the only part now missing. I did nothing for a while and then slowly I started doing things that required me to use those talents once more. I was amazed at how comforting it is to be creative without the wild fixation of a manic episode. I can actually take a break without being scared that when I go back the urge to do whatever I had been doing will be gone.

Much to my chagrin, and possibly yours, I will be on these medications for many years, perhaps my whole life. I feel so good on them that I see no reason to rock the boat. I have made the choice to be well—mentally, emotionally, spiritually, and physically in every other way—it just happens that the chemicals in my brain are getting a little backup. I could have made the choice to be the *sick* person who needs to be medicated, but that would be a decision that I would regret a lot, so why even go there? I have chosen to *not* be a victim of my condition. I have chosen to make new friends, and to reach out in ways that I never have before. I am amazed that I have met more people here than I ever did in Edmonton. I am now content to just let things happen as they will, and trust that the people I need in my life will arrive right when they are supposed to. I have many friends who are 20 years older than me and I do not think that I would be able to be in their company if I had not made peace with my mother.

Every single thing that has happened in my life has prepared me for the contentment I feel now. I have no regrets—not one. Everything has happened exactly according to plan and I am very proud of the fact that I have handled the challenges well enough to feel this good and to have gotten this far.

This poem, which sums up my journey thus far, was the last poem that I wrote, so I feel it is appropriate to use at the end of my story. I wish you well. I wish you health. I wish you the strength to make good choices. From my heart, to yours—God bless.

HAPPINESS—WHERE ARE YOU?

I used to wonder where happiness was-
I searched and searched in vain.
I scanned the faces and eyes that I loved
And explored the surrounding terrain.
No luck had I-it's all a myth,
No happiness to be found.
I went inside to search my soul,
Not knowing just where I was bound.
The walls were lined with cobwebs
And reeked the stench of neglect.
No wisp of air; no sign of love;
No life could I detect.
For years, I sat in darkness,
I floundered and gasped for air.
I waited for someone to find me.
I waited for someone to care.
So tired of waiting for rescue,
I started relieving each shelf
Of the cobwebs, dust, and garbage
That I had gathered and heaped on myself.
The cobwebs were sticky and wanted to stay,
The dust was thick and black.
The garbage was heavy and painful to move-
No matter, I made my attack.
I cleaned until I thought I would drop,
Some told me to let the dust lie.
I knew that I must keep working
Or I would choke on the dust and die.

Marilyn Avient

With power anew, I continued to clean
The corners and shelves of my soul,
To uncover the me, that was, and could be,
Had become my ultimate goal.
One day I saw a sparkle and shine
Where dust had formerly laid.
I wept glad tears for my triumph
And rejoiced in the progress I'd made.
My eyes, by then, were used to the dark,
So long had I been without light.
While toiling I discovered a window
That opened to a glorious sight.
I saw a glowing, glittering world
So alive with wonders to see.
My eyes were able to focus
From light that was shining from me.
I used to wonder where happiness was-
I searched and searched in vain.
I found it living within me
And hiding under cobwebs and pain.

ABOUT THE AUTHOR

As a medical lab technologist successfully handling high-stress situations every day, the last thing Marilyn expected was to end up on a psychiatric ward battling bipolar disorder. But that is what happened in 1984 to this highly successful career woman, wife and mother.

Over the next three years, Marilyn was hospitalized for a total of 15 weeks as she struggled to keep her life and family together, despite the debilitating effects of hospitalization, medication, and the loss of her medical career. She'd always been a perfectionist and a high achiever—as a child she was a consistent honors student—so she continued to pressure herself to excel. Despite her illness, she became an award-winning Avon sales representative, collecting accolades and enjoying a fleeting illusion of success until that career came to an end in 1987.

It took another decade of sustained effort to move from surviving to thriving; thus, she found the material for her five books. Writing had always come easy to Marilyn, but it was not until 2002 that she recognized her passion for public speaking. At that time she began presenting her story of recovery, hope, and life lessons to appreciative audiences.

Marilyn and her husband, John, live in Nanoose Bay on Vancouver Island. They adore their two dogs, Ceili and Newton, and enjoy frequent visits with sons Sean and Jason, daughter

Lindsey and their five grandchildren, all of whom live in Alberta. When not writing or traveling, Marilyn enjoys gardening and spending time with her husband.

Printed in the United States
95984LV00003B/4-102/A

9 781421 899756